Burn:

A Bipolar Memoir

SHANE FELDMAN

TRAFFORD
Canada ▪ UK ▪ Ireland ▪ USA

Note for Librarians: a cataloguing record for
this book that includes Dewey Classification
and US Library of Congress numbers is
available from the National Library of
Canada. The complete cataloguing record can
be obtained from the National Library's online
database at:
www.nlc-bnc.ca/amicus/index-e.html
ISBN 1-1420-2188-x

TRAFFORD

This book was published *on-demand* in cooperation with Trafford Publishing.
On-demand publishing is a unique process and service of making a book available for retail
sale to the public taking advantage of on-demand manufacturing and Internet marketing.
On-demand publishing includes promotions, retail sales, manufacturing, order fulfilment,
accounting and collecting royalties on behalf of the author.

Suite 6E, 2333 Government St., Victoria, B.C. V8T 4P4, CANADA
Phone   250-383-6864   Toll-free 1-888-232-4444 (Canada & US)
Fax   250-383-6804   E-mail   sales@trafford.com
Web site www.trafford.com
TRAFFORD PUBLISHING IS A DIVISION OF TRAFFORD HOLDINGS LTD.
Trafford Catalogue #03-2737   www.trafford.com/robots/03-2737.html

10   9   8   7   6   5

TABLE OF CONTENTS

INTRODUCTION 5

THANKS AND LEGAL DISCLAIMER 7

PROLOGUE 9

WEEK 1 OF JUNE 2002 25

    PART I 25

    PART II 37

    SOME OTHER PART 41

    LOVE PART 45

WEEK 2 OF JUNE 2002 50

    PART I 50

    PART II 58

    PART III 64

WEEK 3 OF JUNE 2002 83

    PART I 83

    PART II 101

    PART III 120

WEEK 4 JUNE 2002 125

    PART I 125

    PART II 130

LAST WEEK OF JUNE 2002 148

    PART I 148

    PART II 156

    PART III 157

    PART IV 161

    TO EMILY 166

TRIBUTE TO MY BEST FRIEND 167

SAME DATE AS ABOVE DIFFERENT SUBJECT MATTER 168

LAST WEEK OF JULY 2002 169

    PART I 169

    PART II 170

    PART III 172

FIRST WEEK OF AUGUST 2002 174

    PART I 174

    HURT – BY TRENT REZNOR 177

EPILOGUE..179

INTRODUCTION

I've worked on this book for two years. In the end I decided to keep the text intact. I decided to leave the work as written from June to December of 2002. I left all the good and the bad to give an accurate account of mania. If I had changed the writing to create a better piece of literature I would have compromised the manic mind. The memoir chronicles a manic episode and the prologue, epilogue, and notes represent the road towards self-discovery and recovery.

The prologue is written in structured prose as an explanation of myself. When I wrote this section I was recovering from mania and beginning to make sense of what had happened. Now I look at the prologue and I see my sincere effort to make myself appear normal. I see more than ten pages with too much detail. But I see something that was written while in recovery; something that was written not only to help the reader but to make myself understand that I was more than the manic episode. I hope that this section gives the reader a better understanding of where I came from before I had the mania.

The body of the book, written in free-style poetry, is divided into weeks as chapters. I wrote in free-style because my thoughts were unstructured and spiraling. I was in so much pain; I was not sleeping or eating. I stayed up nights on end, I would go into rages, and I would hurt myself. During this section of the book I'm totally at the mercy of the illness.

I added footnotes to some of the verses. In the months following the manic episode I thought that the free-style poetry would benefit from some explanation. I believed that my poems could be misinterpreted or not fully understood. At the end of many of the verses is a number. That number can again be referenced at the bottom of the page. I only attached notes to verses that I thought showed a particular aspect of the disease or my personality. In addition I tried not to slow down the text by adding footnotes that repeated the same idea. Therefore, I might show the same trait or symptom over and over again (in the text) but I only identify the idea once. The reader can choose to use these notes or to read the memoir as it was originally written.

The epilogue, written in prose, explores my path toward recovery. I become more coherent. I'm able to understand myself and use this understanding to articulate my growth. However, I still show the remnants of the feelings that I express during the free- style poetry. For example, I show my obsession with Emily by writing a whole section analyzing her current life situation. I used the epilogue to get out all of my feelings of hurt and abuse in a more coherent way. I end the novel with a good understanding of myself, my mania, trauma, and bipolar.

The reader should be wary that not all my actions and thoughts are those of a person suffering severe symptoms of bipolar. Many of my actions and thoughts are normal and many people have and will be able to relate to the different ways I felt. One should not consider her/himself to be bipolar because of the ability to relate. In the free-style poetry section of my book I express dozens of different emotions and actions; I would be more worried if someone could not relate than if someone could understand some of the feelings. The person who cannot relate would seem numb (to me) which can be a symptom of depression. I was manic and depressed, but I was also a twenty-two year old interacting with all the complex issues of modern life. I believe that many people will relate to a lot of what has been written and find comfort in company. I hope that this book not only lends light on a somewhat misunderstood psychological disorder but also provides interest, compassion, and solace to the reader through exploration of the elements innate to all human beings.

THANKS

Thank you, thank you for considering reading this book. Thank you for just picking it up and looking at these words. I have much love for anyone who has an interest in me and/or my writing. I established my web site (listed below) with the sole purpose of making myself more accessible. I hope to help, inspire, entertain, and teach. I hope that anyone willing to help does the same for me.

A book is never created by just one person. I would like to thank foremost my girlfriend, Karlín. She is my reason for living. She also edited this book twice. Second, I would like to thank Shervert H Frazier. He has saved me from myself; by showing me myself. Without him, this book would have no sense of perspective. He is a great man who has helped many. I would like to thank my parents. They provided financial support and kind words of support. I would like to thank my two sisters because they show me so much love. I would like to thank all the good people at www.Animal57.com for helping to make a great site; make sure to check it out for the whole story, www.ShaneAFeldman.com. I would like to thank Margaret A. Liversidge who edited parts of the prologue and the first week of the memoir. I would like to thank Joel Shamas, my lawyer, who helped explain to me how I could write this and not get sued. I would like to thank Eric Kulin from Kulin Photography. He did a great job making me look better than I actually do, both for the cover, and for my web site. Last I would like to thank William Tapply and Don Davidoff, two well-published authors who helped show me a little of the writing world.

Legal Disclaimer:

Although all the emotions I undergo throughout this work are true, some of the aspects of the story had to be modified for legal purposes. The book was written over a period of seven consecutive months, however, the months were not June of 2002 until December of 2002. Likewise the events depicted in this story did not all happen during the same time period, however, my mania and recovery did occur over the time period specified in the previous sentence. All the names have been changed and many of the characters' personal traits have been changed. Furthermore, many of the situations and events are slightly modified or changed. This has been done in a sincere effort to protect private citizens, institutions, and myself from legal action. This is a semi-autobiographical memoir. For more accurate information about my life please visit my web site at www.ShaneAFeldman.com.

PROLOGUE

NOVEMBER 2002

My first childhood memory is throwing this rock off of a big hill in my friend's backyard. I'm lying. The truth is, I can recollect what happened in the seconds before I threw that infamous rock. My mom stood, hands on hips while her best friend (who was also the parent of my accomplice) stood likewise; my mom shouted something like, "Stop throwing those rocks or you won't go to the playground!" I looked at my friend and I threw another rock.

The memories from that time in my life consist mostly of being given various warnings by my mom, such as "You're going to hurt yourself, get off that," or "Put that down before you hurt someone else." My mom was not giving me so many directions because she was overprotective or because she was stern or mean; she loved me, she was being a good mother. The direction my mother gave me was due entirely to her dedication and love. She was a great teacher who taught me everything. I loved her very much. I know that because of the way I treated her. If I fell and got hurt, I ran into her arms; if someone strange came too close, I nestled into her body. I can remember laughing and seeing her face near me. I can't remember laughing without her there. I needed her and I know I loved her.

I loved my dad too. I know I loved my dad for much the same reasons I know I loved my mom. I would throw a tantrum every day my father left for work. I can still feel how warm his body was when I would lie in my Spiderman underwear on his bare chest. On the weekends he would put me in a child seat on the back of his grass-green bike and take me to the store down the street to pick up groceries; I thought he could ride the bike so fast, I thought he was so strong. I can remember trying to do the stuff my dad did, like putting together the broken pieces of a table in a basement that smelled like mildew.

I cannot remember my mom being pregnant with my first sister, or when she was born. But I do remember spending time with my sister when we were both little. We lived in this big blue house with blue shag rugs in a neighborhood in a town on the outskirts of Boston. We moved into that house when I was born in 1980 and we left in 1985. Those years passed by very quickly. I was totally innocent in those days, playing in the sandbox with a bright red plastic shovel, frustrated that my hands wouldn't move with the ease of an adult's. That house's backyard abutted my aunt and uncle's backyard; they had two children, both born in the early 1970s.

My first sister, Mikel, was born in 1982. I loved her too. I know I loved her because I tried so hard to teach her. I taught her how to climb and how to throw. I even pretended I knew how to read. I used to read to her from a big child-size book that I could rest on my legs, with the tips of the book towering over my head. I can remember the first time I made my sister cry. I forget what I did but I remember my

9

reaction. I felt so bad about what I had done that I began treating her like something fragile, something precious. Not all my memories from this time are great, but most of them are. Both Mikel and I got unique names, but by the time our other sister, Rebecca, was born in 1985, I think my parents were too busy with the two of us to come up with another creative name.

I love my parents and Mikel just as much now as I did then. My parents have done nothing but try to create the best life possible for me, and I thank them for it. Mikel and I have forged a loving relationship that has endured throughout all of our life changes. I also have a loving and caring relationship with Becky. We are still all together and under one roof, my two sisters (except when Mikel is at college), my parents and me. When I was in the blue house, I lived a relatively normal life and I continue to live a relatively normal life. I can't remember much about moving from the big blue house. I was five. I remember some packing and I remember the day of the move; the bags were packed and we were leaving but the cat was nowhere to be found. My cat Tiger had run away and we were driving around the neighborhood calling his name. My mom and dad started yelling at each other and Mikel and I laughed in the back seat; the cat was spotted and we all laughed as my dad chased after him, first down the sidewalk and then out of sight. Eventually he came back, red-faced, holding Tiger in his arms.

For the next three years we lived in a little yellow house. I can remember a lot about that little house surrounded by big pine trees. I started school, and I can remember hating it. I had such a hard time making friends, and I had such a hard time doing the things that the teacher told me to do. I was lonely. I never learned to like school, even in college, but eventually while living in the yellow house I made friends, a few, maybe three or four and one really good friend.

Some scary things happened too, though I didn't realize just how scary they were until I was older. I can remember this kid throwing a chair at the teacher during class, and someone else who needed an adult to be around him all the time. I felt bad for these children who couldn't control their feelings but I didn't interfere. I have never needed an adult to put his or her hands on me to settle me down. I tried to play sick a lot, but I never got into either a physical or a verbal confrontation with a teacher. At the time, of course, I didn't know that I would someday be on the other side, as a human services worker helping children with severe psychological and behavioral problems develop skills to feel better about themselves and their lives. In the course of this work I have had a child hit me with a chair more than once; I have also been a "special," a human services worker who does specific one-on-one work with a kid who has serious violent tendencies.

Another memory from that period was that my friends and I loved to listen to "Parents Just Don't Understand" by The Fresh Prince and Jazzy Jeff, while jumping up and down on my family's blue sofa. Later, one of my friends played a scary song from that CD that my parents had told me not to listen to. I had nightmares and I would scream in the dark night for my mom and dad to come run into my room and save me. They did. Eventually the nightmares went away.

As my friendships developed I seemed to become closer and closer to one particular friend. I made my first best friend while looking for toads in the gutters that surrounded our neighboring houses and together, we started a role-playing game based on the movie *Goonies*. My friend always played the character named Mikey, and I was Data.

I got so immersed in this game that I started signing my work at school as Data Feldman instead of Shane. This was not a quickly passing phase. Data remained my official name until sixth grade, and everyone—my teachers, my friends, and sometimes even my parents—called me Data. I don't think this name change helped my social position. In the woods, however, when I was seven and I was fighting against the girls who also liked to play there, I thought Data was a pretty cool name. I don't think the girls even knew we existed, much less that we were waging a fearsome battle against them for a piece of territory that we considered to be rightfully ours. In reality, I think these girls just came into the woods behind the houses to play. Every time they came, we thought they were participants in a covert operation to destroy our forts. I am still embarrassed to think about how I acted then, and my face turns a darker hue of red as I think about how lame those forts must have looked. Those girls never destroyed a fort, but it was still fun to pretend.

I am Italian and Jewish and my friend Mikey had moved here from Iran. I have since forgotten his real name, but it was not an American one. I also must have seemed strange with a name that referred to a gadget junky from a corny 80s movie. I guess he and I would probably have been called the dorky kids at school. I don't think that when you are a dork you know it. Mikel, now in 2002, calls herself a dork all the time, but she's not. When I was young I never thought of myself this way, but my name was Data and I had only one friend. Dork or not, I thought I was cool, and I had a lot of good times over those three years.

One incident that I remember well was when my parents had their sex talk with me when I was six or seven. It was not because the talk was so poignant, or that it gave me a necessary understanding of human sexuality. I already knew what sex was. Instead, my most vivid recollection of the conversation was how uncomfortable my parents were talking to me about sexual intercourse. I had never seen them look uncomfortable before. To this day, and right now while I am writing this passage, I have a grin from ear to ear thinking about how goofy my dad was and the hand gestures he used. That's a very funny memory.

We got our first dog, Pumpkin, in that little house. She was a beautiful miniature sheepdog. She was orange and white and Pumpkin used to cuddle with us when we would watch Friday night television. The dog was de-barked and that always made me sad. I could not imagine what it would be like if someone took away my ability to speak. Then, one day, I heard a screech of tires and my mom came inside looking upset. She said, "Shane, don't go outside!" Later my parents told me that the dog had been hit by a car and killed. I understood what it meant to die and I cried all night in my room. Mikel did not understand what it meant to die and she kept on holding her hands around her neck and sticking out her tongue making gagging sounds. She thought it was funny that the dog was dead; I can remember going over to her and almost hitting her, but I didn't. My parents tried to explain death to her, but she was just too young. The next morning my mom made me eggs and I knew they came from something that was alive. I imagined blood in the eggs and I could imagine how much blood there must have been all over my dog. I couldn't eat any type of meat. I became a vegetarian, and this, like the name change, was no short-lived phase; I remained a vegetarian from age seven until I was twelve or thirteen. I cried into my pillow for days and was very sad for months after Pumpkin died. To this day I can't stand the thought of anyone around me dying. Since then I have had two other animals die and I cried for days after each death.

Of all the things that happened while we lived in the little yellow house, the most important event was the birth of my other sister, which happened not long after we moved into the yellow house. I can remember my mom's belly growing and me putting my tiny hands on it to feel my sister kick. When Rebecca was born I went to the hospital with Mikel and my dad. We all put together Disney puzzles until I got to see Becky for the first time. I can remember everyone in my family crying, even Mikel, and I began to cry too, but I don't remember why.

Now the kids outnumbered the grown-ups and they knew it. My parents began implementing various new disciplinary actions to prevent a mutiny by Mikel and me, and Becky would be strapped down all the time. I think that is what happens when you get to the third child: you have to resort to any means necessary to maintain order. Despite this and the death of my dog, however, Mikel and I had a lot of fun for the rest of the time we lived in the little yellow house. She thought I was a god and followed me everywhere and copied everything I did. If I played a sport, so did she. If I hung upside down on the jungle gym, so did she. Once I told her to grab a bee and she did, and my mom got really pissed when it stung her. But I loved my sisters and could never imagine maliciously hurting either of them. Once I was roughhousing in the backyard garden with Mikel, who was a bit of a tomboy, when Mikey came along. Seeing us, Mikey joined in and tried to wrestle with her also. I think he can still taste dirt from my furious assault. I think I made him bleed. I have always tried so hard to protect my family, and my family has tried equally hard to protect each respective member.

When I was eight we got a new dog, Indy, and with all of us getting bigger, we clearly needed a larger house. Since my dad was making more and more money by this time, he and my mom decided to build a nice big house in a very exclusive suburb. When I was born we were lower class; now we were upper class, with my father earning though not seeing a hundred thousand dollars a year. We still live in the house that we built then, though much has changed since we moved in. Now we have a swimming pool in the backyard and a circular driveway. Most of our original neighbors have moved away. The tree in the front yard, once shorter than I was and held up by posts and wires, now rivals the house in height. Now I enjoy where I live, but the move was hard on me. I wanted to live in the movie *Goonies* for the rest of my life; I wanted to be one of the carefree characters who went on fantastic adventures everyday. I also wanted to have a best friend next door to accompany me on those adventures. I had to settle for retaining only my adopted name, Data. I can remember hiding in the bushes of the little yellow house when it was time to move.

Changing schools was a terrible transition. Despite that one situation where Mikey disrespected my sister, he and I had grown tremendously close, and I did not want to leave him or the comfort and security of my old neighborhood. The new neighborhood kids were not very nice to me. I ended up fighting each one of them. The leader of the neighborhood kids was this tough guy who would brag about his martial arts experience. He was one of the first people I ever fought against. He used to beat everyone, often doing all kinds of exotic fighting moves during school. One time, I faced off against him in front of his kid sister, who encouraged her brother by telling him to "tear Shane's face off." I beat the hell out of this kid in front of his sister and earned the respect of the neighborhood and the school. My respect was short-lived, however, and I was still very shy and reclusive. Soon after this fight, new, faster-talking older bullies arose. I ended up fighting against most of them too.

I did not like to fight, but I was very good at it and it seemed to be the only means I had of boosting my social status. I was not academic enough to warrant attention, nor was I particularly good at sports. Fighting, however, made the other kids excited; it made their blood rush and it drew their attention to me. I had to fight as often as once a week just to prove that I was not stupid. I had poor verbal skills, and the other children would ridicule my inability to maintain a fluid conversation. I would often leave words out of my sentences when I spoke, as I did in my written assignments. As a result, people didn't always understand me very well. I was a sensitive kid, and the hazing that the others did to initiate me had a major effect on my psyche. During that first year in my new school I became very nervous, very insecure, and very easily distracted.

Fortunately I was never caught fighting by a teacher and I hardly ever got disciplined in school except for poor grades. School continued to be very difficult for me, and many people thought I wasn't trying. My parents, however, always tried to help me with school, both by working with me themselves and by arranging for tutors to coach me. On the recommendation of one of my tutors I underwent a psychological evaluation around the time of my ninth birthday. As a result, I got a label of having a learning disability. I was also told that I had anxiety which contributed to my speech and academic problems and that I had short-term memory problems, a poor attention span, and general language problems.

Eventually I ended up getting average grades, and as the first year passed at my new house I began making friends. I again got very close to only one other child while having three or four other friends. His name is Jack. A few times the neighborhood kids pushed him around and I made those bullies pay. I can remember playing football with Jack and my dad, the smell of pumpkins in autumn, the family all squeezing together to watch *Full House* and *Family Matters*. The sense of family togetherness was strong.

After another year I was fully integrated into my new school. I was a pretty average kid. My grades were not too good and I had the occasional peer conflict, but I was pretty normal. Both my sisters were old enough now to understand just about everything. Mikel and I still had a very good relationship, but Rebecca did her own thing.

I am not going to give an introduction to the next part of my life because I was not given one. It was not a typical stage, and there was no way it could have been anticipated. I am not going to grace the reader with fluidity because to me this part of my life is a series of detached, nonlinear memories. Something terrible happened to me when I was around ten: I was raped and tortured on several occasions by someone I trusted. I do not remember how many times. It was so terrible that I cannot remember most of what happened in my life from ages ten to sixteen. All I can offer the reader are the fragmented memories of a series of incidents that happened to me. I discuss these incidents later on in the free-style poetry section of this book.

The first sign of my descent after the incident was that my grades began to falter again. I started getting Ds, so my parents, whom I had told nothing of what had happened, sent me to a private school from seventh through eleventh grade. In trying to grasp hold of memories of this time, like a child chasing a butterfly, I remember when I started writing poetry. I think it was in seventh grade. My teacher at the time had been published and had also received a few teaching awards. After she read my first poem she pulled me aside and said that she looked forward to seeing me get published someday. In her class I found that I loved writing, and I have never stopped. This was the first class that I ever got an A in. I can remember one of my friends thought that he was a great writer too, and subsequently he got a B+. My friend couldn't understand why I got such a great grade. He wrote a lot of drugged-out hippie stuff that he thought was insightful, and my writing seemed to him all drugged-out too. My poems were shorter than his, and he thought they made even less sense. I think we were both perplexed about what made good poetry, and to this day I think there is only a fine line between brilliant poetry and a talented poet on drugs. My best poem was Really: I can do a flip/ But I still land on my back. It was a good poem, I think.

During the years that followed my trauma I can remember trying to maintain a relatively normal persona. I had a few outward problems, but I have never been arrested and I never hurt anyone besides myself. Even at private school, there were many children with more apparent mental and behavioral problems. For instance, some of my peers were engaging in unprotected sex and going in and out of rehab for drinking or using drugs, but I never used any drugs, and from the time I first had consensual sex, when I was sixteen, I used a condom.

Even so, inwardly, I was not doing very well; I simply was good at hiding my problems. I had flashbacks of the rapes that made me feel embarrassed. As a result of my feelings of humiliation I sometimes felt angry and hateful and at other times sad and worthless. Through my parents' relentless efforts at trying to help me, however, I was able to make it through tenth and part of the eleventh grade. They did everything from buying me a puppy to sending me to a psychologist. They got me the best tutors and personally made sure I made it through all my classes. I didn't make many friends after I went to prep school, but I maintained strong ties with Jack and we did practically everything together. My sisters both did better in school than I did, which did not help my self-esteem. As a family, though, we maintained our integrity. Every year we would do a variety of family activities, not because of tradition, but because we really did love doing things together. My sisters and I developed more mature relationships. During those five years that I

14

spent at prep school I tried to help my sisters whenever they would fight with my mom and dad and lock themselves in their bedroom. I can remember that they tried to help me under similar circumstances. We still help each other.

Then at sixteen I fell apart. I refused to go to school, and my parents sent me to McLean Hospital, a famous mental institution, as a day patient. Each day from October 1996 to February 1997 I drove to McLean and spent six hours in the adolescent program, and during my time there I was diagnosed with severe depression and anxiety. I would not tell anyone—my parents, my therapists, my friends—about the incidents of rape and torture until several years later. I can remember a lot about the day program, from the layout of the building to the dead eyes of the gothic kids. I can still see many of those patients in my head when I close my eyes. I can see these young people coming in to the program stating "I'm already dead," from the White Zombie CD, and leaving saying "I'm going to try," with renewed confidence. We used to play CDs in music therapy, and that is where I first got to listen to Korn. I enjoyed their music, but it was not until a few years later that I heard the lead singer sing about his own experience with childhood rape. I could relate, not to the exact incident, but to the tone and the manifestation of his words. I rarely ever left the program until 5:00 P.M. because all the real therapy happened when the staff was no longer around. We talked about how we were getting better or worse, and I found that the patients were more insightful and had developed better coping skills than most of the staff. I tried my best to help them and most of them did the same for me. I will not spend too much time writing down how much I cared for those people because I do so again within the free-style section of the memoir that follows. When I left the program, I cried the whole drive home and many of my friends inside the program cried when I left. I hope that they are doing well to this day.

I have always cared for other people. When I was in my early teens, maybe twelve to fourteen years old, I helped my grandfather deliver food to the sick and the incapacitated. I know what it means to take the time to sit down and talk to people who are destitute. I know how much people depended on my grandfather for social support. When I went to the hospital I spent most of my time helping myself. However, during every moment I could spare I was trying to give to others. I sketched many drawings to cheer people up. I wrote them poems. I played pool and ping-pong with them. I listened late at night when the residential patients called me collect from the hospital. I offered solutions to those who asked. I even stole from my family to give to those whom I felt were impoverished. In retrospect I see that I probably should not have stolen from my parents, but I did what I thought was best in the moment. I decided while I was in treatment that I wanted to make a career out of helping people. There is no better feeling for me than to see someone smile because of something I have done.

Later, in 1997 I started school again at a special needs high school that served about sixty adolescents, all suffering from mental illness but in some stage of recovery. No one was ever restrained at this school, but you were automatically expelled if you were violent towards another student. If I remember correctly, only two students have been expelled for physical violence in the twenty-five years of the school's history. The school has a 95 percent college acceptance rate, and some of the students are accepted at Ivy League schools. As might be expected, I experienced a period of adjustment as I made the transition from the hospital to the school. In the hospital you could say and do what you wanted when you wanted, and there was only a limited amount of academic work. I had a lot of catching up to do. I can remember trying to use my mental issues as an excuse to do less school work, but the teachers would just look at me and say, "Go to class or you won't get enough credit to graduate."

With time I began to make a commitment to academic work, but I learned more than just academics at this school. I learned how to interact in a more positive way with people. I also had my first girlfriend, Kim, whom I dated for several years. She was incredible. I can remember spending hot summer days at the beach with her and the cold nights of winter lying next to her. I can remember making cheeseburgers on the grill in the summer with my arm around her waist, and the taste of potato salad and lemonade. The air was so clean, and at night I could hear the crickets chirp and the low droning sound of the air conditioner. The beach was nearby and the air smelled of it. Kim's mom worked all day long, so from 1:00 in the afternoon until past 11:00 at night we did whatever we wanted to. I remember soft kisses that tasted like "Juicy Fruit," the smell of her perfume, and hot baths. I lived with her for weeks at a time. I would say good-bye to her mom and then crawl back in through the basement so that I could hold her tight all night. Season after season our love grew. After I graduated from high school, however, we went in separate directions and could no longer maintain a relationship. I swear that I have not had a good night's sleep since she slipped through my arms.

I had begun my new high school at the end of 1997 and graduated at the beginning of 1999. During that time I had a lot of exciting experiences that were new to me. I can remember sneaking out late at night to see Kim and going to parties with beer and people throwing up before they made it to the bathroom. In addition, I made a very good friend at this school, my first true guy friend, with whom I talked about adult issues. We used to talk about everything from girls to music. I also became friendly with nearly everyone else at the school. I found that I loved peer mediation, and I used to try to help out the kids who were not that popular, because all of a sudden I had become so popular. I knew how bad it had felt to be unpopular or generally disliked.

My sisters were growing up and beginning to have boyfriends while I was going through high school. They helped me so much during all the times I faltered; I can only hope that I gave them one-tenth the support that they gave me. For the first time since I was ten I began having fun again, going to movies and nice restaurants with my girlfriend and traveling to all kinds of fun and exotic places with my family. My family and I traveled all across the Virgin Islands. Eventually we visited all the Caribbean islands from Aruba to Puerto Rico. At one point I went to Disney World with my girlfriend and my family. My mom gave me another talk before we went about the reasons to wear a condom.

My next-to-last semester of high school was good. I joined the yearbook committee, not because I wanted something that looked good on my college

16

application or because I had too much spare time, but because I loved photography. All throughout high school and junior high I had loved taking pictures. I guess I figured out my love for photography around the same time that I developed a love for poetry, but photography was far more expensive and I had a hard time gaining access to a photo lab. Later I joined the prom committee as I wanted to be able to show my first love a great night.

Graduation became imminent when I started school in the fall of 1998. I already exceeded the credit requirements and only needed to take a few more mandatory classes. I took my SATs and my SAT IIs. I got a 1200 on my SATs and finished between the 35th and 45th percentile on my SAT IIs, scoring slightly differently on each of the three subject tests. At this time I also enrolled in a college class at a community college, where I received an A- in a freshman-level English class. After graduating from high school, in January 1999, I began working for my father, installing voice and data lines for his telecommunication company. I was happy. I had no big ups or major downs. I fought with my family over what type of car I would get and where I was going to college. The small stuff. I got into Clark University in Worcester, Massachusetts. Besides having an excellent psychology program, Clark is small enough that I could be more than a number.

I left for school in September 1999. My mom cried and my dad looked more upset than her despite his lack of tears. I hugged both my sisters and told them that I loved them, and then I went off to college. Despite the fact that I made a good start academically, I lasted only a few months. I had many discussions with the Dean of Students, but I could not handle the social elements of school. When I told the Dean I had decided to leave she gave me the opportunity to come back whenever I chose to.

I worked until January 2001, when I went back to school for a semester. During those eight or nine months I continued to live a happy life without psychological incident. I continued dating Kim for the first few months of 2001 and we had many great times, but we finally broke up. We fought hard to maintain the relationship. We tried to get a relationship therapist involved and I tried to get an apartment closer to where she lived. Neither method worked. In the end we realized that although we had both grown up, we had changed in different ways and were no longer compatible as a couple. We cried together for a while and decided to remain friends.

Around that same time I got my car modified. I started saving up money to put into projects I was interested in, though it seems that I always ended up wasting a lot of it. I poured maybe ten thousand dollars into that car and I never saw any of it back when I traded it in. If my father had known how much I spent on the car he would have had me killed. Besides work, my other main endeavor was writing. I was pumping out two or three pages of poetry and prose per day, and I also began organizing my past writing on the computer. I am pleased to see that a lot of it is quite good.

The school that I went to in January of 2001 was a local college called Lasell, which has an excellent teacher-training program. I was considering becoming a teacher because I knew how much my teachers had helped me in high school. I did well, earning a GPA of 3.925, and I would have gotten a 4.0 if I had not fought with my English teacher so much. I think one time I made her cry. We began arguing about whether or not society needed laws. I thought society would flourish without laws. She said the opposite and stated her argument as a fact. I continued to tell her she was wrong. She began bringing in scholarly work that proved her point. I began discrediting her material and providing contradictory scholarly material. Over the course of time my teacher must have personalized our arguments. I just wanted to have an intellectual conversation and felt a little sad when she became teary-eyed.

While I was at Lasell I turned 21, and I began going to Las Vegas. During the period of three or four months when I visited Vegas I experienced my first manic episode where I gradually lost my ability to exercise good judgment. It was on one of those trips that I experienced my first full-blown manic episode during which I lost all judgment and was psychotic, spending one hundred and twenty thousand dollars in two hours on a stripper I had just met. I didn't want to have sex with her; I just fucked up.

When I came home from Vegas I was devastated. I felt as though I had betrayed my parents' trust. I felt like I had acted in a manner that was not myself. I did not understand how I could lose myself for so long. I did not understand that I was capable of such poor judgment. I ate barely anything following my return from Vegas and I tried to overdose on Klonopin. I almost passed out and my father called my doctor, who indicated that I had not taken a fatal dose. I was sad and hopeless. Eventually after several weeks of severe depression I entered a psychological day program at a hospital other than McLean.

I gradually showed progress in the program. The doctors, whom I once again did not tell about my childhood trauma, did not change my earlier diagnosis of severe depression and anxiety. They felt that I had been depressed and anxious when I was in Las Vegas, and that I had needed the stripper's companionship and had wanted to impress her.

The doctors' explanations seemed to make sense until another traumatic situation occurred. A few weeks into the program I was sexually assaulted by another patient. He was a police officer and I had no reason not to trust him. He ended up inviting me to his house, where he expressed sexual feelings for me and then assaulted me. I told the staff at the hospital and he was removed by the police to another unit. Several months later he was on the front page of a Boston newspaper after being arrested for one count of sexual assault and two counts of physical assault. I did not press charges against him because I was scared. After he assaulted me, I began reliving my childhood. I left the program and began feeling angry and betrayed by society. Sometimes I felt like it was my destiny to be raped and tortured again and again. I felt like everyone was going to hurt me.

After leaving the day program I fought with everyone constantly. I felt like everyone was out to get me. I got into verbal altercations with my parents that would end with me throwing something through a window. I drank heavily, often driving drunk. I began carrying a knife for protection. I began to feel like all men were going to try to rape me. I was scared.

My parents showed their strength of character by not kicking me out of the house. I told them about the police officer but not about the initial incident when I was ten. I was still too embarrassed. The fighting and drinking came to a point where my parents told me I had to get help. Finally they convinced me to enter McLean Hospital's residential evaluation and treatment center, the Pavilion. I agreed to go because I cared about my family. I hated myself.

I spent two weeks of July 2001 at the Pavilion, where I got the diagnosis of bipolar. The doctors believed that my mood swings, from depressed to angry to feeling as though I had a hundred thousand dollars to spend, were classic symptoms of bipolar, an illness where the afflicted person suffers fast, unpredictable mood swings. (For more information pertaining to bipolar, consult the epilogue.) Their assessment was that I had a type of bipolar that was drug-induced, in this case by the antidepressant medication Paxil, which I was taking at the time of my manic episode in Vegas. Apparently it is not uncommon for people to have a drug-induced mania due to taking an antidepressant, specifically SSRIs, a group of medications that includes Prozac, Luvox, Celexa, Zoloft, and Paxil.

I was put on lithium, a mood stabilizer that is the most frequently prescribed medication for people with bipolar disorder. Mood stabilizers are usually considered a must for bipolar people so that they do not have to feel uncomfortable emotional highs or lows. I did not stay on the medication for long, but I still recovered. I mended my relationship with my parents through outpatient visits after my discharge from the Pavilion. I still felt too uncomfortable to talk to anyone about my childhood trauma, however, and I did not share this until the summer of 2002, after writing the free-style journal section of this book.

Eventually I began seeking outpatient care less frequently and I got to enjoy some of the hot days of the summer of 2001. During the late summer I met and began a relationship with Erica. It was a good relationship, very passionate, another beach relationship, but it didn't last. I was afraid of commitment, and a part of me was probably still waiting for Kim to come back. Now, when I think of Erica I think about the cool autumn breeze and the smell of our fires. I think of when the air went cold and my emotions followed the weather. I broke up with her because I was afraid she would leave me first, but I soon ended up missing her and realizing the folly of my action. She quickly began dating others, however, and I could not convince her to love me again.

Now I am openhearted and ready once again to be involved in a serious romantic relationship. My first two loves are gone, but I will find another to love even more. There was a third serious relationship that I discuss in the poetry. Her name was Emily.

During my relationship with Erica, an important opportunity arose: I got the chance to do what I had always wanted to do, which was to help people. One day in September 2001 my dad came to me and told me about a school that was looking for volunteers to serve as positive male role models. I can remember the first time I visited the place. The people who gave me the tour stressed how the children would act out. The children ranged in age from newborns to fourteen, and about half lived in the school's residences. I was not fazed and was quick to indicate my desire to begin as soon as possible. At the same time I decided not to return to Lasell for a second semester.

I began doing volunteer work that same month, and the first thing that was said to me by the first child I met was, "You look like Dopey." My head was shaved and I do have big ears. I laughed and she apologized to me. Later in the year, when she graduated, she made a speech that made me cry in front of about three hundred people. The work came naturally to me. On the first day I memorized all the kids' names and where their seats were. This was quite a feat because to this day I still don't remember most of the staff members' names. Adult names always come and go, but with the children it is different. Soon I would know the full name of each child in the entire school.

I volunteered there for hundreds of hours. Each time I caught a smile from a kid I would know how well paid I truly was. I got along well with the girls, but the boys really took a liking to me. One boy in particular came into school one day dressed like me; I was so proud that I could have this much of an impact on a person. He grew so much at that school, both socially and academically, and during the school year he ended up being adopted. Subsequently, his academic work improved enough that he went back to public school.

There was another little boy of note who wanted to emulate me. He used to tell me about all the bad things he did. The list got so long, I had to make my own written list to relate to his social worker. I tried to teach him that it was not okay to hit women or staff. But when he was in control of his mouth and body he could be very funny with his sarcasms. Once he made me laugh so hard that I asked the rest of the class to move on to their next activity in another building while I just sat there and laughed. I would have probably let him get away with murder compared to the other kids. He could not help his cursing; all I could do was tell him, "I don't want to hang around with kids who curse." I also tried to teach him the difference between an offensive word and a very offensive word. He called me his best friend. He used to always say, "We're best friends, right?" I would say yes. This child needed constant adult support in order to not attack either another student or a member of staff. He already had a bigger sexual vocabulary than I did. I tried so hard to get him to study in class. Not long before he graduated from school he said to me, "I'm a jackass, right?" and I was just honest and said, "We're a couple of asses." We shared one of our last laughs. I think we (the entire school staff) had an impact on him, and I hope he will retain some of what I taught him. Maybe he will still struggle in school, but he has a bigger bag of coping skills to grab from when he gets the urge to be assaultive.

Each one of those kids has some attribute that makes him or her exceptional. For one it might be the ability to do math at a high school level, for another the ability to relate to other people better than an average adult. I still have each one of their drawings scattered around my room. One day after I work for long enough, I will have a pile that reaches above my head.

I kept on volunteering there until June 2002, when I got a paying position. When graduation came at the end of June, it was so difficult to say good-bye to those who would not be back in the fall. I sat in my room afterwards and cried into my pillow all night long. It was one of the hardest good-byes of my entire life.

That same month I started to feel unusually agitated and angry, yet at the same time productive and motivated. I thought I was angry because I was lonely and that I was feeling productive because I was fueled by the sense of satisfaction I got from working with children. I never thought that I might be manic, but this was, in fact, the beginning of my second manic episode. It was during this period, which lasted for six or seven weeks during June and July 2002, that I decided to write this book. My original premise was to present my insights to the world. When I am manic I feel closer to God; sometimes I believe I have godlike powers. I thought that my insights were so profound that it would be a disservice if I did not share them.

A dangerous incident also occurred during this period that resulted in my hospitalization. I came up with the idea of a photo shoot where I would cut myself in order to show inner angst. I ended up getting cut so badly, both by myself and by the friend I did this with, that I almost bled to death. I have never cut myself with a razor before and in retrospect I can understand why many people would consider this action totally insane. After I cut myself I went to sleep for several hours. When I woke up I was lying in a pool of blood. I felt dizzy and nauseous. I was able to stumble into my parents' room, where I told my father to take me to the hospital. Although I knew that there was something wrong with me throughout this period, it was only after my injury and subsequent hospitalization, first at Massachusetts General Hospital (for about six hours of medical treatment) and then at McLean Hospital (for three weeks of psychological treatment) that I gained enough insight to determine that I had had a manic episode. This, in fact, is typical: every bipolar person I have ever met has not known that he or she was in a manic state until after the episode has passed.

As in the past, I did not mention my childhood trauma to the doctors at McLean, and I stated that my injuries were entirely self-inflicted. The three weeks at the hospital did not help me very much, and I left feeling only slightly less depressed. I felt a tremendous amount of shame and guilt over cutting myself and thought that I would never get a chance to work with children again. Although I did not feel suicidal, I felt that I would never again have any fun in my life. In the last week of my hospitalization, however, I met an incredible doctor named Shervert Hughes Frazier Jr., who requested a visit with me shortly after my discharge.

During that visit Dr. Frazier confronted me with his belief that I was lying about the injury. He suggested that I may be part of a cult with homo-erotic overtones and that I might have been cut by someone I had been having sex with. He concluded by stating his belief that I had a severe childhood sexual trauma that played the paramount role in my psychological problems. He also connected my two manic episodes with the presumption of the childhood trauma as an antecedent. He was very insightful and for the most part, he was accurate as well. He backed me into a corner and, finally, I told the truth. After I revealed my childhood trauma, he told me that I was using the friend who had cut me to inflict pain on me similar to that first abusive incident. He told me that the childhood abuse was still affecting me.

After my conversation with Dr. Frazier I showed improvement much more quickly, and in the weeks that followed I was able to gain a tremendous amount of insight into my illness with Dr. Frazier's help. Most of the information in the epilogue and the author's notes are derived from his therapy. He helped me understand that I was not a bad person and that I could get better. Eventually in September 2002 I went back to work at the special needs school, where I have been doing good work for the kids in my classroom. I have also been writing a lot, working on my first novel.

While recovering from this second manic episode, I looked again at the writing I had done in the midst of that episode. Some of it, I thought, was insightful, but most of it was not. As a result, I reduced the length of the book, trying to keep only the parts that are insightful or that offer a useful portrayal of my manic thoughts and behaviors, as well as my other psychological problems. I have left the book in chronological order so that the reader gets to ride the emotional rollercoaster in the same way that I did. I did, however, shortly after the completion of the book, interject a few short notes to indicate a connection between a thought or a behavior and mania or that would otherwise help the reader to understand more clearly what was happening. I also had to change or modify names, places, specific dates, and some situations to avoid exposing myself to legal problems. I assure the reader that though I may have changed some details that my emotions are the same. I hope that my artistic integrity is not compromised and that the writing does not appear contrived. I have tried my best to retain all the ardency of manic rushing thoughts despite my need to edit it in a minor way.

To further clarify my book I have added footnotes. The notes can be found at the bottom of many pages. Each comment matches the number below the specific verse. I added these comments to convey how someone of a normal mind frame feels while recovering from mania. I also added the comments as a tool for the reader to use to help understand what exactly was going on behind each one of my actions. Each comment is dated as well; to show the time elapsed. One can choose to read with or without the footnotes. I do not have a recommendation. For some, the commentary might lend much needed light into my complex thoughts and behaviors. For others, the commentary may slow down the plot. Others may choose to only look at the commentary on certain verses that are particularly complex or personally interesting.

My intention in sharing these writings is twofold. First, I hope that through being able to read my manic thoughts, people who are not bipolar—including friends, family, and treaters of those with this disorder—will gain an understanding (or improve their understanding) of why someone may act in such a disturbing manner. I believe that in order to understand a bipolar person, it is essential to understand the actual racing thoughts, which offer far greater insight into the condition than can a textbook or even someone's reflective thoughts about a previous manic episode. I hope that through this memoir, readers will gain insight that will help them in their own lives and with relating to and understanding those who are bipolar.

Second, I have written for others with a bipolar diagnosis in the hope that it will offer some degree of comfort by seeing some of their symptoms mirrored. Bipolar is an illness that may cause good people to do horrible things and thus at times, to experience deep shame, but with help they can, not only maintain their stability and function at complex tasks, but lead successful and satisfying lives. I hope that people will find solace in the fact that I am successful despite the fact that I have had manic episodes. Many people who have this disorder not only prosper but accomplish great achievements. The majority of successful people I have met in business, the arts, and other fields have some sort of severe psychological illness, usually bipolar; however, society almost always hears about the disasters related to the condition. I believe that bipolar people are more apt to achieve social and financial success than psychologically stable people, but I also think they are more prone to suicide or other dangerous incidents like the one I participated in this summer of 2002. Bipolar people look at the world in a different way that usually leads to a more creative life, and they often get into highly productive states for prolonged periods of time. For example, a successful bipolar businessperson may stay in a hypomanic phase (an elevated mood that is less extreme than mania) for an extended period of time, perhaps working seven days a week with only two or three hours of sleep per night. There are varying degrees of manic states and everyone who has this diagnosis has the illness in a different way, but we are all treatable.

Bipolar people go from one emotional extreme to another and, many times over the course of an episode, engage in actions or behaviors that are viewed as crazy. I hope that, as a result of this book, people will understand the complexity of bipolar disorder. I hope that friends and family of those who are bipolar will understand that there are rational reasons why someone is manic or depressed instead of dismissing a bipolar person as being crazy. I hope that some of the doctors who treat bipolar patients read my memoir and approach their patients with a heightened level of understanding and compassion. I hope that bipolar people who read this book will feel comfort in the fact that I thought and acted in a peculiar way but was able to make sense of the actions and recover. I have often heard people who are bipolar talk about feeling that they are just crazy. I want to explain to everyone that bipolar people, despite the severity of the symptoms, still have hope for a good future like mine because there are reasons for their episodes that can be understood and actions that can be taken to avoid them. I want to let people with similar experiences know that they are not alone.

I have tried in this prologue to show that, despite my abuse and hospitalization, despite my bipolar diagnosis, I have in many ways led a normal life. I love my family and generally did well in school and socially. I can remember the pain when my grandfather died when I was eighteen. I can remember sneaking vodka from my parents and refilling the bottle with water. I remember crying at sixteen when a girl I had a crush on rejected me. I am a dynamic person who loves to write. I am usually working hard at a good job and engaged in a variety of healthy activities. I go to night clubs and, usually, unsuccessfully, try to meet women. I have been manic as in the pages ahead only twice in my life.

Each one of us navigates the rivers of our thoughts throughout our lives. Sometimes they are dangerous. The chapters that follow tell of times when I have acted on my own dangerous thoughts. In the midst of these thoughts and experiences, when I tried to see the shore from my own swiftly moving river, I could barely discern that solid ground; what was real was so far off in the distance that I lost sight of it in the turmoil of the behaviors I was acting out. In these chapters, you will be confronted by the uncomfortable emotions, thoughts, and actions that I have experienced while manic. This is me in a manic state. Some of the feelings I express are normal, but the actions that result from the feelings are self-destructive. Some of the thoughts that I have are purely self-destructive and some of my actions seem arbitrary. I do not want everyone who reads the book to think that they are bipolar. All people think offensive thoughts like the ones in these pages. Nor do I want people to think that all people who are bipolar are the same. Some of what I have written is insightful. All the religious references are sound. I think some of my perceptions while in this state are very good. I do believe that my mania led to the development of many good insights into religion and society. All people get really upset but most people are able to keep themselves from hurting themselves or others. In the pages ahead I was unable to keep myself from becoming hurt.

In the final section of this book, the epilogue, I offer a reflective look at that turmoil, providing insights that I have gained in therapy, from books, or from shared experiences over the months since the events took place. That section will also include a fuller explanation of the bipolar diagnosis. I suggest reading that section first if you do not have a basic knowledge of the disease, although I think the book is more compelling if read in the order presented.

There is nothing that you can give me
That I cannot take from others.[1]

WEEK 1 OF JUNE 2002

PART I

I have layers and I am unclear. I hold back and I lie.
I have waited a long time opening and
Closing many documents on this computer;
        Hoping that I would be sparked to burn again.
I knew that I could become brighter than ever.[2]

My convictions, opinions on this mixed society
Have rooted deeper into my mind.[3]

My disdain goes on, as the sun goes off into the trees
To hide.

I am bipolar.
My axis one reads:
Bipolar type 2 mixed type, anxiety disorder.
I got this diagnosis from the best doctors in the world
At the Pavilion which is a program inside
McLean Hospital.
The Pavilion is arguably the best
Psychiatric program in the country.
The average stay at the Pavilion is two weeks for
Thirty-five thousand dollars.
During the two weeks you go through extensive testing
To determine your ailment(s).
I needed a few extra days because
I had trouble surrounding medications and trouble
        Forming an outside treatment team.

---

[1] 11/13/02: I think these sentences represent the beginning of my mania. I felt grandiose; a condition where one feels a surge of power and control, often also feeling euphoric. [2] 11/13/02: I was feeling impatient and confused. I wanted to start a writing endeavor but I was impatient while also feeling confused about what would constitute a good start. [3] 11/13/02: I was mad at society, a place where I often felt I did not fit in. Additionally, I believed society was a conglomerate of bad ideas congealed together to create an uncomfortable living environment for anyone.

I stopped taking the medication a week after
Leaving the program
Which was a year ago.
I stopped seeing all but one of my doctors within,
Five months of my discharge.
I have been doing very well since my discharge
Which was one year ago.
I have been in a close relationship with a loving woman,
I have been in a bad relationship with a bad woman,
I have been doing some volunteer work
At a special needs school
And I have been working on a separate book
About modern religions' effects on society.
Over the last year I am not sure whether I have become
Manic or depressed
        And if I had, the cycles were not intense.
At this moment I am becoming manic,
I can feel the surge of emotional intensity
I can feel the flooding, I can taste the salt water
The need to drink twenty beers and buy
A plasma television.
My past trauma is passing like a hawk over my head
        And I will explain that too but my mania comes
And goes seemingly for no reason
Following no time line.
My past trauma on the other hand
Plays a somewhat more consistent role
        In fucking up my life.

When I left the hospital
I had problems taking my medications
Because they prevented
These episodes;
I stopped seeing the doctors -
They told me I needed to take medications.
I would like to think that everyone understands
What I mean by "episodes" but I do
Not think that everyone understands
The rudiments of bipolar illness.
I would think that everyone is either bipolar
Or is close to a person with that disease
Because bipolar seems to be a very popular diagnosis,
Though I am going to briefly explain
        What I mean by "episodes."
I am going to give my dry quick breakdown:

One type of episode is a state of mania
And the other episode is a state of depression.
When I am manic I am happy, wide-eyed, painfully high,
Like I just won the lottery.
When I am depressed I am sad, I do not wake up,
I hate myself and everyone else.
A true manic episode lasts two weeks or more
And a depressive episode lasts, also,
      Two weeks or more.
A depressive episode always (to the best of my knowledge)
Follows a manic episode.
There are people who get hypomanic,
Which is not quite as bad as mania.
      Still others cycle real fast,
Reeling back and forth between
Being high and being low or being low and being normal
Or being normal and being
      Manic, there are many types and subcategories.
I usually get manic for several months
With a depressive episode matching
      The duration of the manic episode.
Drugs are given to prevent these emotional swings
But many people, myself included,
Do not want to give up the "high" of manic episodes.
I do not care about the imminent "depressive cycle,"
All I can see is the vacant seat and
The ticket in my hand to board the thrilling ride,
I am bound for excitement and adventure.
I will fly high, so high I will touch the tip of the faded moon.
If I get sick or fall off, fuck it,
At least I felt something for sometime.
I view myself as at a creative peak.
Some people would think differently and
Depending on whose vantage point I will
Either become better or worse over
      These next few months.
An example of my behaviors becoming better is that
I am capable of writing
      And sustaining going to work at the same time.
An example of my behaviors deteriorating is that
I find myself leaving
      The mall with more stuff that I just don't need.
I think though my psychosis creates fog,
When I have felt like this I have
Spent one hundred twenty thousand dollars

In an hour, on a stripper.
When I have been depressed I have tried to kill myself by
Overdosing on medications.
I did not have fun spending the one hundred twenty grand
But I do think that it is funny.
Now I use my energy efficiently.
I know that I will only intensify and my writing
And pictures will follow me
To my higher level of enlightenment.
I have increased my job hours to at least 50 per week
So let it begin,
The rapture protects me from the horrors of reality.
I can see it coming, the infinite energy,
I will not sleep nor will I eat.
Like last year when I got straight A's
While going to Vegas each weekend.
This time I will not fall into a social trap.
Fuck the strippers and the female internists.
I have a story to write.

I have written other memoirs
First I wrote Shane1
Which pertained to my frustrations around breaking up
With my girlfriend of two years, Kim.
The memoirs following the break
Became my first substantial written endeavor.
I was nineteen when we separated.
I hit the keys and produced the work of a maniacal lover
        Who was fixated on revenge.
Books on angry lovers have been done so many times,
I moved on.
After Kim and I worked on reforming the relationship
So I wrote Shane2.
I never had the stomach for a role as a manipulating whore.
During the next year I wrote both Shane2 and Shane3,
While we still dated.
We broke up when I was twenty and I began work on Shane4.
I met Erica at twenty-two
At around the same time I began my first novel
And stopped writing daily logs.
Now I am twenty-two and
I am planning to write a book confined to this month.
I am going to write, as I feel and as I react,
I will be in the moment.
I am going to put forth my memoirs of my mixed-type mania.

I will put you behind my eyes
but I am going to concentrate harder on letting you touch
And hear what is going on inside my heart and my mind.[4]

Before I begin my shameless self-indulgence
At my indulgence's expense,
I would like to proclaim my movement.
I hope to think in rhymes
So that my writing has some type of fluidity.
Not unlike what I have found in the last three years
Since beginning my organized
Endeavor into study.
(Whether reading by myself or in the classroom.)
My opinions hopefully have ripened
As my understanding of myself
Has become sharper than the razor
I use to both peel the fruit and cut
Pale skin or artificially tanned.
Bloodied as I am, I still stand healthy in word
And ready before a world
Formed by a society created by a society created
By fast food and businessmen;
Who pride themselves on money for
Movement.
So here we all are. [5]

I have learned nothing of something
From my past relationships,
Which is to say
I have learned that what I felt was true.
I kicked the brick wall and
Could not break it down, my ladder broke before I
Climbed high enough to just see over the top,
But more importantly
I have learned from my life's other adventures.
I would wish to bore the audience
With a detailed account of a relationship
Based on a stupid premise;

---

[4] 11/13/02: I was beginning to feel increasingly insecure. I compensated for this loss with grandiosity. A conflict had arisen between my feelings of grandiosity and the realities of life. [5] 11/13/02: I wanted to make clear my goal to tear down the existing moral ideas. I believed these ideas were created by who I thought to be heathens, businessmen. I was happy because I was beginning to feel like I was providing good insight for a positive social change.

As to hope to confuse myself away to a happier time,
Proving
That the newest most pertinent event,
In respect to my disposition
        Is what pains me to tell.
And the above-mentioned feelings of self-hatred
Are in fact, only, maybe a
Result of a girl.
When what I really want
Is reflected by my attempt at making something.
I wish to feel inspired and reborn through my pen.
I wish to make more sense by producing
Decipherable abstracts.[6]

Emily entered and
The only regret I have is that I wasted
A fraction of a fraction of my life's limited time
Doing nothing with someone whom I felt nothing for.
That is a lie, I do not regret that incident
And I do not have only one regret.
I have a million regrets.
I have a million letters tucked away
In my room so as to gracefully
Let sweet song soften my love's intention.
I regret not giving my letters to Emily sooner
And ending something I never wanted
To begin.
I wasted on her from the beginning,
Giving chase to an illusion.
        I'm an idiot…[7]

She would fain a tear in reference to my above statements,
But in reality Emily is the shallow teenage bitch who
Reflects to me everything I hated
And therefore functions as an outlet,
So that I can plug myself into eternal ECT
(Electro-Convulsive Therapy).

---

[6] 11/13/02: I felt castrated by the women who had hurt me. In order to re-establish my manhood I expressed a desire to find power elsewhere, i.e. through the insight of the book. [7] 11/13/02: I was lonely partly because I was hypersexual from my mania. (Hyper sexuality is an above- normal desire or a need for sex; not necessarily with multiple partners – but a desire to have more orgasms or sexual sensations.) The hyper sexuality, in part, resulted in a desire to rekindle my relationship with Emily.

I identified with the abuser.
She was someone who fucked me and manipulated me.
She hurt me by hurting herself
And by putting me in dangerous situations.
Emily is Steve.
Fuck that,
I was not punishing myself or identifying with the abuser.
I was pleasing myself,
It feels good to fuck a thin legged eighteen-year-old.
Eventually I gave in to her, giving up
On all that I hold sacred and deciding that the
Time had come for me to proceed into the masses
As a like part.
I would get married to the rich girl
Who told me of a great love
While she, as expected,
Was unfaithful and addicted.
She having been a beauty most impressive to the world
With a tongue, platinum to my society's gold standard.
She is a slave to the idiocy that I so profoundly reject.
She is a slave to the trend of promiscuity,
She cheated on me more than once.
If she loved me so much,
She should not have needed to go down onto her knees and
Cried saying "Sorry I hooked up with another guy."
She was a slave to the trend of drugs, when offered she
Experimented with heroine and with cocaine.
She fucking lied to me and when she told the truth it was late
And I swear
I tried to make it work.
When Emily said she would be faithful, drug-free,
And get help
I believed her but eventually she just left me.
I think that is how it happened
        Though I am far from sure.
At the bottom, which is more aptly called the center, lies
My ability to procreate and produce a half-wicked legacy.
She was a whore of the media.
She was also a whore, a product whore, an attention whore,
She was my anti-Christ.
I to this day perpetuate this relationship for two bad reasons:
        One, because I need the hurt and two,
Because I am soft for her.
And now I lie to her profusely as if to band-aid the fact
That I need her, I need her to hate me.

I need the gash to bleed
But I need the cartoon character band-aid
        To cover the severity.
If she knew I hated her then
Maybe she would be broken in two for all she gave.
She thought she had given. Thought she would grieve.
She would not care…
She was a shallow cunt
Who could never love anyone but herself.
My manic obsession burns brighter,
Brighter like the swaying flames from candles
That surround the tub while we fuck.
My love and hate get confused as diffidence takes hold.
My actions are to fuck if she calls,
Blame it on a manic impulse.
I can say "I would never fuck her again"
But that would be a lie, I will
        Even though
I know I should not allow myself to be hurt by her.
I need to break that cycle,
I need that therapeutic intervention for a solution.
I knew it, a month into the relationship,
I told those closest to me
That I fucking hated her.
It satisfies me to think that I knew an
Accurate perception into her evil being.
I am pained, however, that I cannot tell her for
        Fear.
Fear that she will run it through her mink, media-born self
And come to the conclusion that I did something horrible.
She would be lost inside a dream
Where she thought she loved me.
She would perhaps believe she loved me which would have been
A coin throw to heaven in comparison to true love.[8]

I spent time with those that I truly love
        And those who love me too.
Zeus's children by mortal women
        Little lost souls – some abandoned.
I don't know how many will make it to adulthood.

---

[8] 11/13/02: I expressed disdain towards a money- and media-driven society. However, I realized that Emily
was a proud member, in fact a prospering icon for what I felt were the evil aspects of society. I wanted her, yet
I hated myself for wanting her because of her connotation.

Hated by Hera.
She tries to kill them
        She drives them insane.
She maliciously reaches her divine fingers down
        In a jealous rage.
She delivers devils in fleshy clothes
        To hurt them.
They grow up fast
        Like all the gods.
From Hercules to Helen, Epaphus to Perseus.
More beautiful but more open to attack.
I just try to do what is right
        But it is hard.[9]

A Pallas young lady and man I will set as Athena.
One is one and all the like in the real myth.
But I must use a variant because I wish to include males.
The true representation of the myth
Is Athena as all the children.
Aphrodite as the nymph of all the sexually virile women.
Hera as all the crones.
Like the bible and everything else,
The triple moon goddess.
So I to will use Athena too be all the children I know.
Males are the sun, the patriarchal societies.
The mother, Rhea came first because in history
Matriarchal societies came first.
        First because men feared women
Because men did not
Understand why women got pregnant.
We thought, maybe the wind, the water,
Eating a bean, swallowing a fly
        And the like.
Later came the sun gods, the male gods.
Everything used to be about women.
The 29 day month was the menstrual cycle.
Women used to select the king
And then sacrifice him after a year or a great year.
Women instituted orgies, bee orgies, cow orgies
        And they would dress the part.

---

[9] 11/13/02: I compared the positive attributes of the children I worked for at school to the Greek gods. I thought the children were very powerful. I idolized the children and being around them made me happy; it still does.

One cult sacrificed their king by having ceremonies
During which a group of drugged out priestesses
Would dress up like mares and tear the king to pieces.
Another society killed their king by
Castration then and then
Left his naked body spread eagle in front of an oak tree
To produce a good harvest season.
Men stopped human sacrifice
And orgies and instituted marriage.
        I think.
I could prove this point were it important to my message.
The three original seasons are based on women.
Like I said above,
The young child,
The sexual young nymph who can procreate
        The crone who is barren.
I am happy to write like this because I am happy to teach.
I teach the children all kinds of stuff
        But this is stuff that I cannot teach them
        For obvious reasons.
Now the stage is set and out will come the actors, the children.[10]

Today in school a young lady named Chloe said
        "How's your girlfriend?"
I said, "We broke up."
        Because to lie to a child is a sin
Misdirection is cowardice or failure to articulate.
She said, "You'll meet another girl soon."
She reached up her little arms to hug me.
Word spread and a young man named Joey laughed and said,
        "Your girlfriend broke up with you."
        "Shut-up stupid! Have you had a girlfriend break-up with you,"
        Chloe defended me.
Lunch came and after Chloe ate her Hoodsie, I said,
        "Chloe why don't you get another ice cream?"
        "I want another too," said another child.
        "No."
I rewarded emotional empathy and let the class see
        What happens when you sincerely care about another person.

---

[10] 11/13/02: I think I wrote this verse to convey the idea that I would call both male and female students Athena. Somewhere during this verse, however, I got carried away and was happy teaching the reader in the same manner that I was happy to teach the children. I hoped that through knowledge, society would be purged of evil and that no more people would have to experience the pains that I experienced.

Love slipped a little away from Emily but my grip is firm
      On giving until I die to help be innovative in teaching
      These young gods how to feel love as a whole.
I would also like to teach them how to trust in the people they love to reciprocate
Their love.

Another day passed.
I got to be happy and comfortable.
I do not understand why I can do what is right
      So quickly for a child
But function so wrong as a man.
I drive home and I miss those children.
In the car I think about visiting a unit.
This Saturday, I should have confronted
      Someone about something
Because I have the power to create something
Better than myself.

I can run real fast through the jungle gym.
The kids are still faster.
I can contort my body and cut through small spaces
But I can never catch one of those kids.
They always choose me to play with.

Athena said, "Do you have a new girlfriend?"
"No."
"Because I was hoping that you could get married
And adopt me."
A wide smile as he lifted up his heavy arms
For a tight embrace.

Fuck, am I fucked.
To write about that and then bang, bang.
Intrusive thoughts,
      Turned into desires.
If I lived at work I would be fine
      I am no one but myself.
I never question my ability to love the children
I work with.
I am in constant fear that I will let them down.
I am a gentle monster.[11]

---

[11] 11/13/02: I was scared that my anger would intrude upon my efforts to help the children I worked for and have a negative effect on a child.

35

I will capitulate if only you give
Me the terms.
Leave a gold coin under my tongue.
At least I will not have to wander this world.
Let me drink and forget, I already wrote my mind.
I wish to forget so much, could care less for Elysium
    If I still have my memories.
I would tell Hades in Tarterus "let me drink
    And not of the water behind the poplar,"
Probably, not a poplar but actually a pear tree
With white blossoms; which would seem more accurate.
I wander around this earth now full of bad memories
I am gratified:
I get the smile
I get the hug
I witness the change, the growth
For those things I am happy.
I am no miserable man
I have a lot inside.
This is the place to put my pain,
Here.
I have plenty of other places
To express my compassion
And happiness.[12]

Emily come home...
I swear I would make a good daddy.[13]

I burn red my brown body turned chrome
    Like an expensive rim.
Torn in half, a sturdy wall protects my thoughts
    From transformation.
Although the thoughts swim round
So far, but only to come back to the same place.
I hate myself.
Pallas Athena save me.[14]

---

[12] 11/13/02: I expressed a desire to die or to at least forget all my bad memories. [13] 11/13/02: I wanted a clean slate by having my own child. That is, I wanted to start over with a new version of myself. I saw Emily as being my means. All three of the last verses were written during the same sitting. In this verse I was obsessing over Emily because I felt like she was a possible solution to all my problems; specifically my loneliness. I had changed from having more feelings of anger to having more feelings of depression. The fast switch between the mania and depression is called rapid cycling; not to be confused with feeling both depressed and manic at the same time, which is called a mixed episode. My tension was mounting though I was still not suicidal or psychotic. [14] 11/13/02: I was begging that I only act in the calm, controlled manner I acted around the children.

PART II

I looked at superchargers for my car today.
For six grand I can get one hundred fifty horsepower.
I will have four hundred seventy-five horsepower.
So it will be done without a thought.
I have a grand.
I also bought this eight hundred dollar pen.
It was impulsive but the pen will appreciate.
I like the pen a lot.
With the car I will be able to go faster than anyone else.
Now I am fast but I want to be the fastest.
That is the action.
The thoughts are abounding
Like leaves under a tree in autumn;
The action is a mouse foraging for food.
Then one day, an unexpected storm,
The tree is hit by lightning
       And crushes the mouse.
My thoughts and actions are both alive
But they are two separate entities.
Now let eyes again lose themselves in my thoughts
That blanket my impulses, blanket my desires.
My thoughts are prevalent
But the action could be described in detail but no
Insight could be gained.
Fuck that I put fifty grand in my fridge pussy book.
That is fucking great that he walked around
With twenty thousand dollars in his socks
What the fuck do I get from it.
       Not that I am not suffering too.
I want more than a pill for my solution.
I want more than to read about someone's behaviors
While manic.
I want something inside a moment,
A reflection loses most of its integrity.
I want through the study of my feelings and thoughts,
Insight:
Into living medication-free and depression-free.
Fuck you for thinking it is impossible.
My wild thoughts in this moment
Are greater than a recap of a bunch of wild events.
I will bore you sometimes
So as to let you know what exactly I am doing

As it is pertinent to the understanding
Of my various afflictions.
But the connections of feelings
And thoughts to behaviors is more important.
The fact that I am human
And like everyone else is paramount.
My ideas apply not solely to an ill population.
My ideas apply to everyone.
So I feel and my perception is:[15]

I fester.
I am rotting.
Sitting in front of a porno
No further than before.
A semester greater
Still in the shadow of my Father's sun-drenched field.
I am behind my world's norms
Wishing my mother had an abortion.
I should not plant, and I should not harvest…
I am so far away.
I am blessed in all the ways which a human can be,
Yet happiness raised one year's spring
And was harvested in the fall
Leaving a dry winter's desert.
Enough has been said about my relationships
And enough has been said to render my book
Unreadable to everyone.[16]

Unlike most
I wrote my story before I released my song.
I better have a good fucking something to come.
At least I was tortured, raped, videotaped,
And in and out of mental institutions.
I suffered enough in my adolescence
And young adulthood to put me in a category
Similar to Mr. Davis, only not so bad.
I am not the dark spoiled kid from the suburbs,
I was never weird,

---

[15] 11/13/02: I was showing two manic symptoms: grandiosity and rage, which commonly are experienced at the same time during a state of mania. First, I wanted material gain as a source of power to feel even more grandiose. Second, I again became grandiose because I felt as though society needed my help and that everyone else was incompetent. [16] 11/13/02: This verse combined with the last constitute a rapid cycle. In the previous passage I had written in a manic state. However, directly after that passage, I felt depressed. In this passage I felt like a burden on society who could not live up to my own innate abilities.

I had a facade that made me from
A distance look normal.
Ever since I can remember, however,
I had outbursts, I am crazy.
I hurt myself and those around me.
All my close friends from high school
        Would tell you I was totally crazy.
Those from high school who did not know me
Would say I was a little quiet and normal.
I dressed and I still dress normal,
What has come and gone is gone.
My actions were my outlet and I had many outbursts.
I am certainly remembered as more than a disruptive kid,
        My behaviors were often violent
And/or unpredictable.
I would pick a fight with the toughest kid in school
One week,
The next week I would walk around, lying,
Saying that I had a pound of weed to sell.
One time I sold a kid fake steroids
And made fifteen hundred dollars
        Before he tried to kill me.
I saw him recently on MTV's *Tough Enough*:
        Fucking dork.
I guess he got the real thing.
I was a medium popular very crazy kid
And after enrolling in a special needs high school
        From ages sixteen to nineteen,
I was a very popular medium crazy kid.

I surmise in the four lines below, the line below,
A particular point alluded to in the above passage:
I hope my youth raped away into porno
Is not on the free market.
I would have smiled more if I foresaw the coming Internet.
Please do not ask me again, fucking whore mother fuck.[17]

I have literally been in therapy for twenty years;
Starting when I was two, my first problem was with sleep.
I was in therapy before I became conscious
Of my own consciousness.

---

[17] 11/13/02: I was angry because I was embarrassed by having had sex with a man.

Through the years my mental ineptitude increased,
Exasperated by incidents
          And by my lack of mental resourcefulness.
I attribute the incident cited below
To my most severe mental deficiencies.
I was raped and tortured by a trusted person
When I was ten.
Ever since then I have been tumbling downhill.
The fall hurts and
I am still violently rolling down my rocky hill.
My clothes have been torn off to expose
A bloody naked man's body.
Anyone who is educated will be able to tell
That not all the cuts
          Are direct results of the descent.
I am hoping that through my last breath of speech
And through the forensics that
Something insightful beyond myself is revealed.

I do not have any fear.
It was carried away on a whisper.
Now my fear is carried on the wind around the world.
No matter where I chase it, it has already been and gone.
Lament...
I am not afraid of death.
To be eaten by the soft-handed Gentile.
I look forward to the nothing
Or the something that is different.
To decay in the belly of conscious existence
Is a destiny I cannot fulfill
Despite being taught of
The Primum Mobile.
The angels' gears of heaven do not turn
With enough force and do not have the conviction
To increase in ardor of inertia
To match my ardent struggle for control.
I am a powerful wedge that will stop the cycle mid-drift
          Causing some of the stars to rain and the others
To simply burn out.
God does not have a rose petal for me.
I will never get to stand in the corona.

I am too pretty to decompose in hell
But with time comes acceptance, beauty fades.[18]

Lament,
The only necessity for anyone to know about me is
To run.
One time a big black man tried to fist fuck my asshole.
One, two, three, starting four the blood poured.
My nanny stayed in my room with me,
Cleaned me up, bandaged me up,
Then he made me suck his dick.
I wonder now if my penis has grown as big as his.
If I find him now it will be worse
Worse than the sour, bitter taste of his
Cum that I swallowed,
Worse than the humiliation I suffered when he forced me
To swallow my own cum.
Now I have become big, big enough to fuck him.
This time his ass will be the one without the Vaseline.
I had to shit out more cum than he did.
Lament…
Here comes the next part.[19]

SOME OTHER PART

The following is my most advantageous dream put into words. My dream stands alone, no mandalas, circles, or squares, no potential solutions to a subconscious problem, no mythical hero to bring me insight and/or strength. My regard for religion stops a second after my pen hits and I do not know how I render any order. I believe in gods/God, I simply have not yet aligned all the pieces. I am not going to justify myself for being explicit in this part. However, I can write something to help give you some insight as to why I have such a vivid recollection of something that can be so easily forgotten or skewed. My detailed account of this dream stems from the fact that I have had this vision so many times. I drag out an instant in order to drag myself and you in, I want you here. I want to be honest with you; I want you to believe me despite my doubtful sketch. I have to first indicate that some details do change from time to time but the basic idea is unfailing. Inside this part is the most detailed account of my most dreadful

---

[18] 11/13/02: My reference to the *Divine Comedy* was an attempt to show my fearlessness. I wrote about not only my acceptance of impending death but of how I would not go to heaven. I felt out of control and the only defense I had was confidence. [19] 11/13/02: I compared my penis size to my abuser's because I wanted to know if I had grown more powerful than him.

dream. Take me as I put myself. What you feel inside you is the truth, do not let change lead you to doubt, there can be several truths and I am often wrong.

I have been dreaming lately as part of a spiral.
There is a dream I have in black and white.
I am maybe eleven or twelve, past innocence but
Before turning culpable.
I walk through a dead land,
To my left all the castles of McLean Hospital;
      Fixed, ever old and architecturally beautiful.
The big brick buildings sprung up
Twisted, swirling, and radiating like grey flames.
All I can hear is this little screaming girl.
The sound violates all my senses.
I enter a hot building, the ivory towers
With the two sculptured lions, Codman House.
Once inside I descend into the overwhelming
Infamous McLean tunnels.
The maps have been purposely squeezed from memory.
My disorientation prevents an organized endeavor.
I move forward under one building to under the next.
I can vividly see moving people.
All the dead souls around me
From all the hospital's history,
Smiling at me.
All I can hear is the little girl inside
Screaming from pain, she is paramount.
Everyone is moving fast around me
But I am moving slowly, eyes locked,
I do not want to wake up.
My ambivalence makes me vapid.
I walk deeper down the tunnels with the brick,
Then the dirt.
The blood and piss in bronze-colored pools
That shine on the floor,
All the suffering souls.
I can see myself from the outside,
Walking unimpeded deeper
Down.
I know that I am lost,
The tormented souls are transparent because
Each limb is moving so quickly like
A solitary flame in winter's
Cold long night.
The images transcend any of my imagined horror.

Everyone suffering is so happy as if having an orgasm.
But youth drowns the impossible expressions
From reality's olive face.
Still the images cause my senses to reel.
The child smiles as an adult would
At the pinnacle of sexual pleasure.
The impossible expression of sexual joy spreads:
First sending the tortured mouth wide,
Second slightly gaping
And finally into smaller O's curving toward the ceiling.
I have a headache from this little girl's shrill screams,
Her dry moaning,
Her squealing.
The dream screams are different
From the open-eyed screams I hear at the hospital
When a child is being restrained
For her own protection,
My vision's screams could tear a diamond man
Into many pieces, these are the
Screams that are caught while the pain is inflicted
For pain's sake.
The sound of suffering, while a predator catches a victim,
Truly, no matter how soft the volume,
The sound hurts the mind, forever echoing.
I come then to a spiraling staircase,
And descend deeper, the bronze fluids
Flowing down the spiraled stairs,
Dripping upon everything but me.
I look to my left always
Seeing a four- or five-year-old girl
Getting raped by an old man,
He pulls out and his men not by force
But by her reaction send her back.
She smiles at me.
Next he begins breaking her into nothing,
Tearing her apart with one hand,
In the other hand a knife,
He is spinning it violently inside her,
A chainsaw to a flower.
All of this happens in fast motion,
But not so fast that I cannot see her smile
Turn perverse
        Comfort
And I can see the blood shot at me but not on me.
Then I slowly move my eyes as

Her eyes roll back in pleasure,
She eventually closes her eyes smiling.
Next I walk the last steps coming to the bottom
Where there is a broken white fridge
With blood and pieces of insides
On the handle.
The noise still draws me like a Siren,
The disturbing visions still vivid around me.
My family including an older matured me
Is standing in front of me
And they look,
I do not desire to confront them.
There I am nearly a thousand feet underground,
Up to my waist in a stew of broken pieces,
A thick broth of blood.
I stop to look at a water strider quickly
Jet off in front of me carried easily on the thick liquid.
I stand for as long as I can stand.
Watching more than five hundred people
Getting raped and murdered.
All children, growing in numbers as my family
All with hollowed sallow white eyes
Just stare straight at me.
Images flailing around in a massive basement
Of human waste, blood, and pieces.
Killing the young, raping them
Till mutual satisfaction.
I neither enjoy it nor detest it.
I only know that I must stay.
Usually I do not sleep enough
To get within talking distance of my family,
But if I am lucky the dream continues,
I look at my present self.
And in a voice resonating the iron taste
Of blood the words "Betray, Betrayed."
In a moment a woman will come,
The decayed image of a once-spectacular woman,
Perhaps Kim.
Fat and covered in maggots surrounded by flies;
Missing clothing, missing teeth, missing skin.
So real that I beg my conscience, conscious of my sleep
To stay asleep.
And I, as an adult, leave with Kim and disappear.
Then my aged self reappears again and another comes
Maybe

Emily.
Skinny with a hole in her belly and her head shaved
Totally naked I catch her exposed vagina sagging,
Just above the soup's line
With hornets exiting to swarm around my family who
Momentarily take their eyes off young me
To watch old me go away,
So very ordinary are the dreams.
Again and again coming and staying.
I had forgotten for a long time,
Maybe six months since inception.
I always have a headache now.
I hate myself for being capable of dreaming
In such a graphic way.
I hate that while asleep I relish the dream.
I hate this dream more than anything
And I would never wish to see any of it.[20]

I added this part to the book because I wanted to let the reader understand that I am capable of feeling as much love as hate. I think I am capable of more love than hate. Though now, my love has shot across the sky and burnt out like a star. And so all I can offer is a break.

LOVE PART

6/01
My heart splits in half.
It hurts,
I am crying.
At twenty-one, standing 100, 2800 away,
Feeling like 1,000,000.
Jess where did you go?

I met this girl in Las Vegas, Nevada.
I fell in love with a stripper.

---

[20] 11/13/02: This dream is explained best in the epilogue. This dream was about accepting the joy of sex while being hurt because if I had not experienced some joy I would not have been able to ejaculate. The words I hear, "Betray, Betrayed," were about challenging my sexuality. I betrayed my heterosexuality by having had some pleasure with a male. The rape and torture that I underwent had a tremendous effect on me. In the verse I was struggling to understand why I had an orgasm with a man when I was not gay. The answer is because people get sexually stimulated by physical actions. For example, a young girl riding a horse may have an orgasm. I was still maturing when I was raped and I could not control my natural reaction. Once I understood that (a few months after I wrote this book), I became a little less angry at myself because I was less confused. I was also less angry at myself for enjoying being hurt. I learned that because I had an orgasm when I was ten or eleven when raped does not mean that I was not tortured.

Right in the middle of a million men in front
A million men behind;
Probably a few girls, a few boys, and some women.
I was robbed for a hundred thousand dollars.
I wonder what Kim would think about Jess.
We only kissed, I gave a little lick,
She took her money and I went home.
A few months ago I went to St. Thomas.
I met this girl there and I kissed her, too,
I did not lick and the age difference was seven years.
Seventeen to twenty-four and it is all the same.

Jess the Shining Star
When I look deep into your eyes
I see the infinity of the deepest ocean
Swimming so fast in thick thought;
My eyes open.

Gazing at one million people you stand apart.
Everyday I walk through the endless seas of faces,
Everyday, like the last, I sit quiet
Watching the sun fall beneath the trees
Igniting them into a hazel blaze.
Next comes darkness and my defeat;
Knowing that even the sun
During its glorious drop from the sky
Is not as beautiful as you,
One in a trillion... my most beautiful princess,
If the heavens were raided
And the future fallen in mid-sprint
I would still not find a radiance
To be onyx next to you as the flame.
And so I swear away, my blood leave my veins,
Do not fly away.
The ladder now also fallen,
I am futilely trying to stop the inevitable ascent.

I am crazy as a strange dream,
Cursing the thin line that connects us,
I got lost, I lose myself to words without vision.
I need to be able to speak myself to you face to face.

Such things matter, as tiny things die
I can visit.

When I arrive, I will open my hands
And give you the moon for a hat,
The stars for a bracelet,
I will be standing before you,
I will be whole,
More than the nervous voice over the phone.

In my lucky world where all the faces smile at me
Yours is the only one bright enough to lead me.
Through your brilliance I arrive at
Refinement and dignity,
Drawn, like a hummingbird to a flower.

My words are tearing and ripping apart
From the strain of a heart filled fat.
I hope that my words from calculated hands
Prove to be finding something searched for.

I want to be wild as a little devil
Jumping off walls and tearing ceilings down.
I want to be funny and true.
I want to be the adult that my experiences have brought me,
I want to be the adult that my intelligence
And honor have earned me
I want to be unmovable in moral conviction and strong.

Beautiful Emily
My head burns
To a bright ruby hue.
I do not believe in creationism or Darwinism.
Perhaps these theories apply to those born alive.
My life is not responsible because of
The cut of a cord and a first breath.
Walking around with a heart covered with tin
I was born as you bore through the metal.
My incoherent ramble does no justice
But alludes to the deep truth:
That I am awkward expressing my deep love for you.
I exude love as a naïve child exudes innocence,
You smell as roses next to the ocean.
Your eyes glow blue as a perfectly cut sapphire
And deep as a cloudless sky.
Your skin as if an angel came down
And touched you with the essence of divinity.

A touch from the tip of your slender finger
Brings someone of a young heart to his knees.
My own hands shake as my pulse quickens
Allowing me to see the ultimate truth of being alive
Through your kiss:
I only am.
My love for you is
Far greater in breadth than the distance
From a pointed index finger
To the most brilliant glowing star
In the clear summer night.
My soul being convinced that you are
The only one capable of healing my clotless
Wound inside my muddled brain.
I need you more than you understand,
More than ten people of great intellect
Left to one device could understand
In ten of their lifetimes.

Kim
I know I have not always been a great friend
But I have always cared for you.
I have always tried.

I had been lost.
I have been alone.
And despite the fact that you have not always stood by me
You have always been at the end.
You have always lighted up a path to something better,
You helped me to grow up and taught me how to be able
To confront my many struggles.

When I felt like shit
And nothing was going in my direction
I turned to you
Because when I focus in on you
I see that there still is something beautiful
In this ugly world.

When things get chaotic you sit down with me, and talk.
You are the only one I ever met
That had the slightest intuition into who I am.
You see and accept me for who I am.

You are a pretty and sexy woman
Who has tremendous talents at art and at understanding.
You have always been able to see things for what they are,
And although no one can see you exactly
I try to understand your personality in all its glory,
But I get caught up in rings of complexity
Deep inside a cave of trauma.

What you have given me in a list
Too long to write,
So in such a small space I struggle.

You taught me how to love.
This is the greatest gift,
You taught me that love is not about sex or holding hands.
It is not about words or actions.
It is a mind frame.
It is a way of loyalty and compassion
That cannot be written or spoken
And now that you have given me this
You can always know how I feel towards you.

As I grow older and our roads fork
I will always think about you as having
The biggest effect on me,
And of helping me the most.
I do not know where I am...
Until I hold your hand.
Your touch is light and shines my way towards utopia.

When I sit and think my thoughts turn round,
And back to you.
When I feel bad my memories lift me.
My memories of you and your energy,
My memories of you make me laugh.

I remember love from laughs.
I remember someone who cares.

WEEK 2 OF JUNE 2002

PART I

Emily,
I look into your big blue eyes like the ocean,
Your blonde hair like the sun
      I watch the sun set for night
To give way to complex darkness.
I should never have let you try that heroin.
I should never have let you cheat on me.
You cheated on me,
You cheated 3 times with 2 different people.
      (At least it is a holy number)
You cheated before the drugs.
      And I still honestly
Wonder if you are doing terrible or are lost.
I thought I had the warmth of the sun but I only got burnt.
Now you lost a beach.
On drugs
You look as a blown light bulb
The darkness fell fast
After the plunger ran its course to collision.
And like the useless bulb
You too looked charred, when I held you
      I could hear the broken pieces rattle.
You inject yourself with venom
Then you bite and inflict me.
Emily is a whore and a liar,
And now she is becoming a drug addict.
What is worst about her is that she is a bad person.
She enjoys other people suffering, sadistic bitch.[21]

---

[21] 11/14/02: I enjoyed the elements of pain attached to obsessing over Emily. Obsession and the eventual repetition are symptoms commonly associated with a manic episode. Otherwise I would not have cared enough to write this passage. When Steve raped me he fused pain to pleasure. I want the reader to take note that the rage that comes forth in these verses was by no means comfortable. I was not trying to be gratuitous or in some other way create a more marketable book. During times of manic rage I would lie in my bed naked with the covers off because I was so hot. I would move the fan directly over my chest and still I would burn with fury. I could not stop thinking about these angry thoughts that would drive me to attack these people in writing. I tried. I would not sleep or eat; my whole brain was overwhelmed at times by these feelings of an all-consuming anger. The rage was like a headache that I could not alleviate.

My throat burns.
My eyes turn cherry like a dessert wine.
My hands are clasped.
My mind is full of thoughts not connected by theme.
Myself is an illusion created by a group of others
And my genealogy.
I was built like the other cars in my class,
I am only slightly different.
I am a piece like the many items I strive for,
I got confused. I feel nothing.

I float above the water.
I do not soar.
I cannot die.
I am eternal as death.
So I am like the dead,
With little validity to my speech, in an inaudible tone.
Someone touched my shoulder lightly
While I was floating,
Even though I did not turn I knew that I was not alone.
There is comfort in something.
There is a fruit atop a mountain in the distance,
Whose sweet flavor will refresh.
Stand still,
I am scared of movement though pain dulls the fear.
I will eventually find a little hole
In the fiber of this world,
I will crawl in and I will corrupt.
Until then lock up your daughter
She is less safe than your worst fear.
My only weakness is the pain radiating from another.
I feel even though he or she is very far away.
Let me be a deterrent,
That is why I have the foreign scribbles
In my chest to warn the innocent.
Take heed, run at my handshake, less let it progress.
You will be hurt.
And from that hurt I will get hurt the only shadow
Of an emotion that I can feel.
My hell would
Not be inside a circle or the bible's definition.
I would have to let people gain my trust only
To hurt them in a way that I cannot control,
That is my only way to experience pain;
That is my only outlet to feel anything intense.

First the intense care for, then more intense…
My fucking things up.
That is my fucking life, all laid out.
Over and over I do this to myself and I like it.
        If you hate me then I love you.
At the first sight of kindness I will run or hurt you
        To hurt me.
I live in hell, God could not construct
A more diabolical prison
I cut and the wound does not hurt,
I get beaten and raped and feel nothing.
I see you cry and I feel debilitating pain.
You strike at me with vicious words
And I feel debilitating pain.
The machine is constructed by my mind's
Need to feel.
I guess my real hell is numbness.

I am stuck in a 90s wet dream,
Wishing I lived in the 80s…
The most hallowed decade.
I am still here, the wind of time affected my body.
I might have lost some things.
My sense of right and wrong are drawing closer,
So that now I just act as I feel.[22]

The clouds float high,
I wish that I was a cloud up in the sky.
I am a rock
Kicked around in a parking lot.
I hope that the flower gets watered
Even if not from my cloud.
I wish to get submerged again lost in
Life and confused.
I know what innocence is
And everyone is still a little innocent.

---

[22] 11/14/02: I dream of the 90s because that was when I had my first long-term sexual relationship. I felt that my first relationship was pure and innocent. People tend to deify their first love because he or she succeeded in creating a new great experience. For most people, their first love is the first person who can help create a physical orgasm and a feeling of intense psychological intimacy i.e. a mind orgasm. I fell in love with the second person I had sex with, Kim. She was the first person to show me emotional intimacy and sexual intimacy. Additionally, bipolar is typically a degenerative disease without being treated; I did not treat my bipolar. Thus, I slowly began having worse manic and depressed episodes as I got older.

Innocence is getting so caught up
In the magnificence of life,
That you can only feel that one pure feeling;
So sometimes if I cut myself
Deep enough and bleed severely,
I get so high and all I can see is that
Red thick fluid travel down my body,
And drop soundlessly to the floor.
Pray let it last 8 hours.
That is innocence,
A pure emotion that transcends
The reality of conscious thought.

Sometimes I would get this way from writing,
But that was when I was young.
Innocence fades and sometimes
It gets cut off suddenly.
Then when you redo your action
You no longer get lost in it.
I want to find an innocent love:
A love where every time
I say hello or even to think of her…
My thoughts run to her
Like a toddler runs into her mother's arms,
My feelings becoming
Congealed into a state of bliss because
She is everything in nothing.
That is love.
To be thinking of her and not know it,
She is beautiful but all I feel,
Are the waves of a perfect emotion.
Like when looking at something off in the distance,
Then making the realization
That you were not looking at anything in particular,
Nor were you thinking of anything specific.
But in place of those lesser illusions
You are caught by love,
She is beautiful but I do not know.
She is wonderful and I know why
But I cannot think about it,
When I see her she will be greeted by instinct,
Rather, than premeditated attempts
To achieve a figurative perfection
She is beyond my ability to imagine perfection.
There is not a goal.

Just the ascension from two to one.
She will feel the same way and I will know
For the same reason I know her beautiful.[23]

Life has a strange change when you stand still.
At one point each of us stands so still
That if a second party was to touch a shoulder
The first party would be cold
Then one changes without thought or provocation.
A world is created.
A world falls and is broken.
I think movement is brought about by death's imminence.
God did not make you in his or her image.
Instead God started the opening of this universe,
To spark into flame a greater fire.
One day we will become greater than God.
God gambled through the implementation
Of death and evolution.
The gamble was to win something better
        Than what God already has.
The gift of death is our greatest motivator towards
Greatness.
Meanwhile God is afraid to die, afraid because
The odds indicate that death will not prove
Enough motivation
For significant evolution and creations toward
The slow build-up of something to surpass God.
People may reach the status of gods,
But God will probably fail.
It is part of God's inherent eternal being
That God is eternally tied to
Failure.
God's failure would be to create a child
That does not surpass their parent.
Eternal patience, however,
Is the virtue necessary to create the greatest entity,
But a restricting quality to one's ultimate
Individual achievement.
If God feared death then God would be quick
To strike away and recreate
Afraid that one nothing would grow greater than another.

---

[23] 11/14/02: I wanted to fall in love while writing this verse because love was a way of numbing myself and making me feel more innocent; I was petrified that I would not find someone. I also tried to control my life by controlling my life's fluid, i.e. my blood.

The Universe would fall and be rebuilt and bore away,
God needs the patience of his
Immortality, the eternal life bearer.
The creation of death was instilled on people
So we would have a reason to grow.
God or gods sit without the shadow of death and
So without that shadow God
Lacks the inclination and ability to run.
If we killed God
We did it a favor giving the supreme entity
Perhaps the only thing
That it could not bestow upon itself.
Death makes us create, develop medications, cures,
Motivates us to live good lives,
To prosper for ourselves and others.
The motivation to build a legacy through
A better generation.
The motivation to grow.

I bought a Mont Blanc
And a little fridge
To store my blood in
So that I can write from my heart.
Pearl Jam sucks:
Politically correct pussies.
I read the bible everyday for fifteen minutes.
I am picked like Moses
But doomed to purgatory
First for 30 times my time spent on earth
In excommunication.

I will be granted flight out of ante-purgatory
But doomed to walk across each cornice
For a time longer than it took us
To become ready for Jesus.
I read now so that I can murder
And pillage the other 1425.
I can read the bible for a month,
Be set for three years, I can be a bad person.
Recant on my death bed (late penance for reasons of war),
Believe in Jesus and go
To heaven.
I am like the cardinal on the tree in front of my house:
      Justice, prudence, temperance, and fortitude.
I am definitely like the three tears I always shed when
I cut purposefully:
      Hope, faith, and charity.
I never raped but I could be called close,
I never molested but I could be called close,
I never cheated anyone, betrayed anyone,
Never had sex with a minor but I have tried.
Never thought of taking the rose
From someone who has not yet bloomed.
I love everyone who has loved me.[24]

Lenny Kravitz sucks:
That trendy fake fucker worse, though,
As pretty as Eddie.[25]

---

[24] 11/14/02: My obsession with blood begins to play a more prevalent role as the story progresses and honestly I do not know the exact origins for that obsession. In this verse I wished to write in my blood. In other verses, blood has represented innocence, my self-hatred and anger, escape, and suffering. Western culture is obsessed with blood. The blood of Jesus Christ is something that many of us drink in the form of wine at masses. I think that blood represented a release to me. All blood comes from the heart and seeing blood was an affirmation that I still had a beating heart. The heart typically represents love or sometimes another extreme emotion. The heart is the center of life in one's body. To bleed heavily you must be alive because your heart must be beating to carry the blood to the cut for it to heal. Post mortem wounds do not typically bleed. By writing in blood, I believe I was trying to transfer my heart's emotional power onto the page. When blood was released from my body I felt sedated and peaceful. I do not think I cut because I wanted to feel pain. I think blood represents liquid passion; all the intensity of the heart brought out of the body in bright red streams. After I was raped I can remember going to the bathroom and seeing semen and blood in the toilet (after I defecated) and I can remember that image better than the pain, in fact I can remember that image better than almost anything else associated with the rapes. Seeing blood was like seeing my life leaving and it reminded me how I was alive. Perhaps in this verse and throughout this book I desired to see blood because of the above listed reasons, and because I learned from a young age how the sight of your own blood could remind you of what it means to be alive and breathing versus nothing. Cutting is a way to control life. [25] 11/14/02: Everyone wants to feel like they are a superstar and I was jealous. I wanted control so that I could protect myself from people like Steve. Also, after one is abused, he or she tends to look at the world differently in the sense that others are now viewed as potential threats instead of fellow citizens.

Sometimes I am right,
Sometimes I only hope.

I have something to say that you can follow, Sparky:
Not here but there, if I close this screen.
Then I select the file 'I am God.'
I have some unique insights to be followed for change,
That are not so apparent.[26]

I wonder if I am now hated, again.
Get one person and I can be hated forever,
Have to learn to be loved again for a lifetime.
Get a million and I can be hated for a day
Loved the next.
The masses dictate a dream
Of forgiveness and morals,
That the individual is incapable of having.[27]

My life is only an again,
Like the many who bitch about
A puddle despite the oil rainbow and the sunshine above.

People are so mean to each other over
Not understanding the other's understanding of something.

I feel like a fucking fortune cookie,
Something that may have caught your eye
But really means nothing.
I hope that I am something, because I am not on lithium,
I am not a satisfied wonderer content at everything.
As a wonderer on lithium
I was impregnable to insult because
        I was not there to receive the rhetoric.
On lithium I saw my change and changed myself…
With a razor from an eyebrow pencil sharpener.

---

[26] 11/14/02: This verse was referring to another document that I wrote when I was manic. While manic and a megalomaniac I thought I was a messenger from God or gods. Megalomania is similar to grandiosity; megalomania, however, is a psychosis (grandiosity is not a psychosis). Psychosis is when a person has a defective reality or has lost contact with it; it is a mental derangement like schizophrenia. When in a state of megalomania one often believes he or she has supernatural powers to help, hurt, reason, understand, etc… I wrote a document called 'I am God,' about a new religion. The document was about fifty pages long. I never finished it, for my megalomania simply left and I returned to my normal life. [27] 11/14/02: I hoped that my psychological illnesses would not over shadow my artistic talents and intellect.

They sent me back
And I got prescribed a new mood stabilizer,
Then I figured my angle
And convinced them to release me.
I had to feign cooperation in regard to medication
Eventually,
I stated that I did not want to take a mood stabilizer
Doctors told me I would fall without one.
Perhaps the greatest medication psychologist in the world
Told me I needed to take a mood stabilizer.
I did not follow his wishes and I am happy because
I do not have the expected
Generic medicinally induced moods.
Without medication my mind is free of obstruction
I am free to try to reach my own truth.
Now I take a benzodiazepine to help me sleep.
I love my klonopin
If I did not have to ration it for sleep,
I would OD every day:
Less stupid than alcohol but just as relaxed.
The thing that I lost forever that I miss most
      And I mean this with all things relevant,
Is my ability to be a teenager.
I miss most being 17.
With 16 being a close second.[28]

PART II

Love is happiness without slavery.
Slavery is happiness
And happiness makes one a slave to the activity,
But love makes no slave.
I could have loved someone,
Got caught up in the sun,
Looked only forward to a sunlit path,
And never have seen
      The storm clouds behind me.
Innocence is the only mode in which one can be happy
And not be trapped.[29]

---

[28] 11/14/02: I wrote about my disdain for mood stabilizers and how I enjoyed manipulating bright doctors to discharge me from psychological programs. When I wrote about the medication I was reminiscing about what and when it felt good to be alive; I felt most alive at 16 or 17. [29] 11/14/02: In this verse I acknowledged my preordained ideals for happiness within the context of a relationship where one party is a slave and the other the master or abuser.

I first felt innocence on a stairway in front of Mclean's Codman House. I was sixteen and I was with people ages 12 to 18. In the white veil of snow with those magnificently diverse young people, I felt for the first time as though I belonged. My heart hurts at the realization that I will never feel that way again. I will never be so enamored with a moment as I was on that lowly front porch. I cannot write anything that would express my gratitude and longing for those snow kissed nights. During those nights surrounded by smoke and words of insight, I manifested into an individual. Everything before the influences of those nights has turned pale and blurry. I was born into my way of thought late on one white night. This poet will perhaps never hold the words nor see them expressed by another in a similar situation to match my ardor of love for those long ago evenings. I will suffice in stating that I will always strive to remember everything from those memories of the last great snowy winter. The smell of cigarette smoke and the stale taste of snow on chapped lips, the inner warmth extending throughout a cold body, and the great vision of snow capped buildings and beautiful people. I will remember much of my first four month visit. I will always remember everyone's name. I will always remember those days as a sweet dream.

Sometimes I hate the way I write.
Despite how much I love writing
And find refuge in my words.
If it sucks real hard,
I feel real bad.[30]

That something stood in front of me.
First I could make out her shape.
Then her face and then the color of her eyes.
While part of her,
I missed the rest of her.
Then I broke the stare and we sat together for awhile.
Next she vanished.
I always think of her
And everyday I look for her,
Everywhere and in everyone.[31]

Adam is one of my names
And when given my helper I rejected her,
        Told her better to keep my ribs.
Better to fuck a goat and not worry about bringing up
        Some fucked up brat.

---

[30] 11/14/02: This passage was written about the previous passage. I felt sad and angry because I wanted to write something good that better articulated my feelings at McLean. [31] 11/14/02: I was writing about a broader idea of love; about looking for the innate comfort that only love offers.

I ate from the Tree of Knowledge
And accept responsibility.
But for some strange reason
God still gives women the burden of child bearing,
I wanted a pear.
I do not think I will live to be 800.
An illusion from a given name, a stupid book,
And an open-eyed dream.

I gave in during the 90s,
Because I always said in torture,
Love can still be plumbed.
Now wounded in the 20th century by her wicked blade
I will not open for fear of a hemorrhage.
Love does not have substance enough to fill me.
Maybe once but not now with the word love sank,
  I know of nothing big enough
To cork that gaping hole.
It is just as well,
The worm cannot penetrate a flawless apple.
  I was swimming
And she threw a brick at me;
I saw it and did not move.
It has been an hour now, and still nothing;
She is nothing and I am something,
Spoken as pathetically as my conviction in it.

I cannot write about what I am doing in the real world.
Which is to say I can only write about the thoughts
  Not the behaviors.
Because I exist largely in these thoughts
And I cannot write too much about
Work at school because I have an obligation
To respect the privacy
Of the children in my care.
Sure, I make bad decisions but only over money
  And it is only my body.
I am a great human services worker.
My thoughts save me
From suffering my bad actions' inherent guilt.
I am sure, however, that I will still overflow
And spill a little action
  Onto these pages.

I remember one of my first poems was written

About a vision I had of Jesus
Crucified by a post stuck up his ass
With all the world's tears for him gathered,
The earth rained
For forty days and nights.
Noah at 600 built the arc
But Donald Trump bought it from him.
Noah hired a whore and was happy
For even in death he was doing what he loved.
Trump only let the strong and some of his friends board.
His kin and the strong run the stock market,
The upper class.
His friends made babies
And they are all the fucked up people, the lower class.
His kin marrying a friend
Makes up the rest, the middle class.
Therefore, the middle class are the only class
Not a subject of inbreeding.
The strong of heart and mind
Are always going to be defeated
By idiots carrying guns, the jocks;
Perpetuating all the religions' ritualistic battles…
Sports representing indigenous battles,
I watch them.
I am blind in one eye.
Everyone can tell even without looking at me
It is strange.
My story is flawed
Because Jesus was born
Several thousand years after Noah
But the image of Jesus crucified
As I described makes me confident that He
Died in enough pain to repent this sour world's sins.
And everyone knows Trump
Is the earthly eternal manifestation of the true devil
        He exhibits enough pride in one day
To make Lucifer look humble.

The night continues and I digress
Further down my spiral until my writing sucks so much
That I wake up the next day
And am afraid to touch the keyboard
But I am back,
I never left.

The sky is painted navy blue from the moon and the stars.
Black is an idea
Only realized in a memory or a black time
Black is the treatment of people during
The Apartheid or the Holocaust.
Black is felt during a moment of violation
Not a category or visual perception.
To consider black as both a color and an evil is wrong
People are people.
I do not know what to call you,
African American, Jamaican, colored
I rue because I am confused as to how to please you.
I repudiate the idea of different colors
Because everyone is the same.
And I am sorry for being ignorant.

I hope that when read,
One comes to thoughts and questions.
No questions for me.
Just for you.
I plied for you and now
I want an act of purgation.
My beautiful princess
Smiles like the August sun.
Body soft,
Soft as marshmallows, sweet like life and alike.
To my senses you act as a rose
The rose lacks your sedulity and grace.
I just met you
In a hurricane of words leaving
A drowning landscape in your wake.
Doing work to help the depraved, you are nonpareil.
I hope only to give you what you deserve
With respect, gained through others' natural revelations.
I see you soon in a point a million miles above me
Taking the sun's place after it erringly flees,
        Embarrassed.
I look forward to feeling your warm light.[32]

I will not write to you pornographically
For I have not met you,
I do not know what you want.

---

[32] 11/14/02: While manic, I felt utterly and painfully incomplete without a lover.

62

So like everyone I wonder if the prospect exists.
Never look down on another
Everyone has problems.
Despite how bad the problem
Everyone is trying their best.
I am confusing and complicated.
If you can read the words on my chest
Then you deserve a moment;
If not you first have to work.[33]

Nothing about me is as perceived
I am an enigma
My only allure is my potential
My potential is nothing.

Fuck,
I mean lament.

I want to spread some skinny girl's shiny legs
And while I slowly slide in,
Place each glossy leg on my shoulder
Until I am inside and you are cheek to knee
Starting slowly and pushing hard, my body to yours.
Next I would begin
Pressing my stomach hard against your area
And at each deepest moment
I will speed up with every spasm pulling almost out
Then speed up again so that I slap you with myself,
With each end movement
Then at my last moment I will not warn you and pull out
Wetting you from stomach to hair and a little inside,
A gradually opening mouth.
And if that does not work for you
I will do something that will.
I will do whatever it takes to get you to orgasm.
I do not care; I will do anything.[34]
Why did last summer have to end,
I did have fun.
I loved you.
I wish those good feelings could have lasted forever.

---

[33] 11/14/02: I was trying to flirt with readers due to manic symptoms of hyper sexuality and loneliness. [34] 11/14/02: As I have written, being painfully lonely for no apparent reason can be a symptom of bipolar. In this section I was hypersexual, I felt like I needed sexual gratification and if not, I would feel worthless.

Instead the feeling tarried away.
I wish I was not so fucked up
I wish that I could have let you put
Gyres around my heart
I just gave up the best thing to ever happen to me.
Why did it have to end.
I wish I could have stayed over at your house forever.
Even though I said I had a hard time there,
I wish I had stayed with you and gotten married
Within your walls.
Visiting you in the hospital,
If I could have intimacy and fun inside that place,
        I know we could have made it work.
We were depressed and damaged and we created love;
In a natural environment we would have lit the world.
Soft skin and a pretty face, long days and starry nights
Watching movies with smiles lighting the room
A laugh to light my soul, your kiss emanates,
Eternally burning away the ice on my heart.

Now everything is gone because I just throw it away
It is my fault.[35]

If you do not like what I have to say
Kill me, I will therefore,
Do better than my presumed positions
As a deformed bush in Hell
I will sit alongside the heavenly paternity
After ascending from the earthly maternity.

PART III

I love the band 'Sublime'
Many people are real with real things to sing,
I do not think that everyone sucks
        There are a lot of good bands
That make me feel the spectrum of emotions
I like 'Pink Floyd,' 'Tupac Shakur,' and 'Trent Reznor.'

---

[35] 11/14/02: This is not mania; both this verses and the last were depressive statements. I felt hopeless; I felt like I had created my own hell. While depressed people can feel sometimes (but uncommonly) similar emotions to mania like hyper sexuality, they usually do not feel emotions of grandiosity or megalomania.

Fear is on the tips of the phoenix's wings
Whose flight will take me to meet our maker.
The earth is a spot that sprouted,
The seed of an expanding universe.
The first to wander, tarrying away into nothing.
On a rainy day when the sinners' tears darken you,
God will breathe heavy hope that through guidance,
Not divinity that folds, will become smooth.
As a young girl sits watching the rain drops race,
Her fixed eyes.
One day she will hurt another and
Her tears will fill a reservoir.
Then someone will drink that water,
And someone will be quenched.[36]

Today is a good day.
You have to be out there to know it,
You had to be getting inebriated,
More drinking less time inside a book,
There comes poetry.
It was nice for you to call.
Fuck you
I hate you for calling me stupid.
I hate all the simplicity of the world.
The droning doting of the bulk of this poisoned society.
The satisfaction at one lazy perception
Without the effort to obtain another;
Sloth has become an ability:
The ability to be stuck between life and death,
Heaven and Hell, you live in Purgatory,
You may suffer long
        But eventually you move,
Maybe to just fall
Or fly then fall or fall then fly or fly.[37]

Emily keeps calling
Even though we have been apart for a month.
I feel bad for her; she has so many problems.

---

[36] 11/15/02: This verse was written during a depressive episode. I felt like my fear of a worsening society would be realized and that I should commit suicide. [37] 11/15/02: The mood of this verse was very different than the last. I am not sure if I wrote both these verses on the same day. I was manic, describing my own grandiose ideas about how the entire universe works.

I think about her a lot,
She was more beautiful than the blooming
        Wild flowers
That are beginning to paint fields
Purple, orange, and pink.
She saved me.
I was something terrible and I
Was going to destruct.
She helped me.
Now I am back to self-destruct.
She was bestowed an awful fate and
I did not help enough.
I sit drunk on Saturday night,
Wreaking of smoke and alcohol.
The taste of beer resonates in my parched mouth.
My thoughts are like mud and my face is on fire.
I shout out in traffic soliciting a prostitute
She was probably a college kid
Heading back to her dorm.
I get home every weekend night at 3 AM
And I lie prostrate.
The pain Emily inflicted was the fuel that made me good
        From a sadomasochistic relationship
Came a human service worker.
I wake up each day and face a classroom of 10 kids
        I love them and I do my best.
Now she is gone and so is my judgment.
Still I sit, drunk with a hard dick
Looking at the girls dance.
My friends decide to fight
        I add another two fists to the 40 - already
Shredding him.
Two days later a kid tells me he has had sex:
        He is 9.
Another incident report that breaks my heart to write.
I do not know whether I am
Manic, creative, or a sociopath.
I could never hurt a child.
I would rather suffer an eternity of pain.
I am on and then I am off.
I do not know who controls the switches in my mind.
I cannot kiss another girl
        I walked away from a group.
But to be tough I scream at the prostitutes
From a safe distance.

I could never have fucked her.
I am clean, I only fucked five girls, good girls,
Except this last bitch.
Fifteen beers a night on a weekend,
Yelling at the Mexicans downstairs
Doing 125 down the Mass Pike on my way home.
Tears while I try to implement
A deescalating behavioral technique on a 10 year old
         I fail and get punched.
I think that all great work was born manic,
They are all just fucking manic memoirs
         Just without the connotation.

The floor moved
I had nothing to say and another person fell in.
One day I hope to watch people climb out
I am sick of listening to their braying moans.
It is cooler today
I feel massadistic, because I am not educated.[38]

I wish I went to college
I wish I got a proper high school education.
The only thing I learned in high school
Was how to act normal
So that I would not end up
Dead, addicted, or in the hospital.
I learned how to interact with others in a normal way.
Then at normal college
I spoke normally and I offended.
I was different from the other kids.
I was more free.
My education was good.
Fuck you.
I am sure I want to fuck some of you
Maybe I want to fuck a person reading this
         With whom I am familiar with,
Maybe I want to fuck a stranger.
Anyways fuck me, call me, or email me if you are cute
Jremh@aol.com or go to my web site
At www.ShaneAFeldman.com.

---

[38] 11/15/02: I felt helpless and depressed. I felt like I could not change what I thought was a troubled world.

The phone may ring a lot
But eventually there will be voice mail
Leave your number.
Maybe we can get together.
Maybe we can have a special relationship
Where I only have sex with you
Like all of my past relationships.
But also like all my previous relationships
You must have another relationship;
A boyfriend of at least a few years
Or one that proposed to you
Or at least the one who took your virginity.
I need to compete because
        I feel whole when I win.
I never cheated even though they did,
Some of them,
I should have known
I made my own bed to lie in, I created a destiny.

I have a hope, I hope that all my past girlfriends
The ones I truly cared for and tried to help
I hope that they all are getting fucked right now.
I hope the person fucking her is someone prettier
And smarter than me
I hope it is someone with a bigger dick than mine
I hope they are moaning, I hope they love it.

I love this society because anyone can exist.
People are free and that is wonderful.
We are all free to run if we want from whom we want.
We can hide and within reason we can strike back.

I could live without money; I would just need stuff
Stuff makes this world turn.
Sure, money is the axis that the world spins on
But stuff is the substance that I need to feed upon.
So I keep chasing stuff and this world keeps spinning.
I can live without money,
Not without food, sleep, air, shelter, water, and sex
I have nothing profound to say.
I was subjugated by sloth to never exude articulation.
I think I got it all out earlier.
I am a reprobate because I left love.
All I want to do now is bitch about things
But I cannot because I know enough

To know that bitching is boring for you.
I have no insights today because I did not see anything.
Republicans suck!
Reality TV sucks because
TV cannot totally substitute my existence -
By creating other people with
More interesting existences,
I have to compete.
But I do not (compete) and by not trying I really win.
I suck, I have a predilection towards sucking.
I need to take a break and find something to say,
I need to see that pretty girl who sparks my pen.
I talked to Emily but her life is just so stupid -
That I cannot gain
The slightest insight into any aspect of life.
Emily is a totally useless boring melodramatic person.
She is nothing,
But it seems that even from nothing I can say something
So I guess that there are degrees of nothingness
And she is
A very small nothing
Compared to the larger nothings that some others are;
I am going to sleep,
Call me
If you have soft thin legs, a pretty face, and big tits
And no STDs, I hate fucking condoms,
But I swear I am clean, so call me
So that I can make
Cum drip down your legs and off your chin
And out of all your other orifices;
Or maybe we will just talk and I will treat you right.
I will never hurt you.
I will try anything to find you
And when I do you will fear death because Elysium
Would pale in comparison
To the magnificent world I will build you.[39]

I have a language problem
That makes it impossible for me to use big words
I cannot memorize another language,
I am severely learning disabled.

---

[39] 11/15/02: This was a poignant example of a mixed episode in a bipolar person. I was angry, depressed, and happy. I was hypersexual and overconfident. However, I was also discouraged and depressed that I could not find inspiration.

Right after I got tortured and raped,
I developed a fucking learning disability.
I am so discursive in my writing
That I stop anyone from developing an interest in
This book's plot development.
That is why I use little words.
I think complexly
And know that I could write things better but I cannot.

My many adventures
Last year from a famous Vegas stripper
        Who has since played
A large role in a popular Hollywood movie.
To the daughter of a billionaire
Whose family owned a professional football team
To the daughter of one of the most prominent
Food chain CEO's.
The stripper had big tits.
But she was iniquity.
The billionaire's daughter swallowed.
But she was an idiot.
The famous CEO's daughter did everything.
But she was beyond evil,
She would have made Jesus
Wish he had lived.
From Vegas to South Beach to Boston, and California.
From 25 grand in Cartier jewelry
To 40 grand in tips, and fake tits.
From Bentley Azures to penthouse sweets.
I am not Puff Daddy, so I have nothing left to say
But suffice that these women all had good qualities.
The stripper cared so deeply for her children.
The billionaire's daughter had a sweetness
And a giving personality that I miss.
The food chain mogul's daughter
Was a phony bitch but she tried to make herself better.

I wish that I could save this world.
We all have a responsibility
And it is my fault when someone commits a crime.
I knew that it was wrong to commit the crime
But he or she did not understand
Why not to commit the crime.
I have an obligation by being educated
To stop people from doing bad things.

I know right from wrong;
Others do not, I could show them,
They cannot learn themselves.
There are so many reasons (beside the fear of jail)
Not to commit a crime
I know it and I can teach it, many do not know
Why one should not commit a crime.
A child does not learn how not
To steal, hurt, or cheat until a parent or another figure
        Teaches them.
Criminals were never properly taught
But it is never too late to learn.
I wake up and I feel bad about the way the world is
I have disdain towards the world
But beyond all the shots I take at society
I want to help society.
I want to help a teenage mother
Without a significant other.
I want to help her child.
I hate myself most for not being able to help more.[40]

I wish for green grass and budding flowers.
I wish for warm days
With smells of cotton candy.
I want everything to feel as it did
When I first rode my bike
I bled for you, but I could bleed more.[41]

By the lesser light of the gibbous moon
Alone, night after night
I do not like my cognizant attitude towards society.

In a black oven I cook myself.
I am getting ready and becoming close to being done
My skin itches a little bit.
I know not why I am, I try to become something
But I come out burnt, I would taste like charred chicken.
I would smoke and set the alarm off.

---

[40] 11/15/02: I was in a megalomania state; I thought that I could change the world. I was not thinking of reality-based situations that I could control. Instead, I was trying to develop ideas to implement that would fix some of society's most complex problems. [41] 11/15/02: I was what people typically refer to as manic while writing this verse. I felt over-stimulated, excited, euphoric, my heart was beating fast, I could actually feel the memories; not just remember. The reference to cutting was psychotic because (I thought) through cutting I could reach a greater high by controlling (what I believed to be) life's essence, blood.

Even though I was put in your oven
I am only as good as the quality of my meat.[42]

The river flows in a circle
Around a blind man
Who knows of the river and so is afraid to move.
The water is teem and
Another lost soul jumps into the river and drowns
Another time the blind man is indifferent.
Hearing the pain but frozen by a fear precipitated by
Something he cannot control.
In the rainy and sunny days time passes
God hands him food, drink.
The man sleeps and wakes,
All the confused souls walk to the edge and try to jump
But are caught by the undertow
Then for a moment the old man is happy
Because he is taken care of.
He knows his place in fear
He is smart not to move.
He is a tree in the woods.
He is that famous person on TV and in the movies.
He listens but never responds, so
A swirling river of floating dead surround him
He does not mind, or maybe
That is what he wants us to think.
The people undeterred by the carnage continue to jump
Even when the time comes
When the blind man is dead and
He is a rotting corpse across the River.

At a point in some people's lives they just stop caring.
There was a succinct time in my life when I did not care.
I read all these books about philosophy and religion
And came to the conclusion
That everything is simply simple.
None of us have control as control is typically defined.
We are blessed to walk through life in dalliance.

---

[42] 11/15/02: I believed that I was aware (on some level) of the increasing intensity of the manic episode or at least that I was going in a downward spiral. In this verse, I recognized the end to the my episode as being death.

We live in a world of a grand illusion
    Only able to think of one thought at one time
    Once the thought is said
It is bequeathed into the void.
The great illusion is that
We have control over our progressions and digressions.
We do have some control
But my definition of control is different from the
Typical or common definition of control,
Our control is manifested into filters.
Obviously not all of the readers
Are going to understand what a filter is
    So let me explain it for you.
My filter was made by school, my mom and dad,
And all the other
    Teachers in my life,
Including those teachers who taught me to hate.
I am conscious of my filter but once my filter is on
    I become unconscious of it's function.
Most of us have filters that give an illusion of control
But in reality those filters get turned on by
An unconscious switch.
I do not ask a pretty girl to –
'Fuck me' because that thought gets caught
In the filter, the filter protects me from being an ass
    I do not think –
'I should not ask this woman to fuck me because
She is a going to be upset
And she will be upset because she might fear
That I am unstable,' and so on and so forth.
There are a book of reasons why we do not do some actions
Yet we do participate in others,
But instead of accessing a book
    We simply act based on our filters.
Our filters change with time
And the influences brought with time.
Sometimes we change our filters at our own device.
Sometimes others change our filters for us.
Mentally retarded people do not have good filters
    That is why one might say
'I want to put my penis in your pussy.'

The retarded person just knows that sex feels good to him.
We (people of average or above average intelligence)
Function on instincts (also)
However, to mask our instincts
        We have filters which
Prohibit us from saying and doing certain things.
We do, all have filters.
Filters are our developed morals,
Subconsciously manifested into systematic responses.
We see something on the televisions and say,
'That is terrible'
And subconsciously we are really interested
In seeing the carnage.
The want to view the carnage is our instinct
And our filter automatically turns on
Because it is not socially acceptable
To want to see violence.
We learned that violence is to be
Avoided and frowned upon by nearly all
        Our teachers.
Most of us know nothing of our subconscious.
I only know a little of my own.
Our actions are instincts,
We make ourselves believe that we have control
But everything has already happened.
Behind each one of our actions
Is an instinct that we probably do not yet understand.
A women might say 'That is disgusting,'
When she is really turned on by the naked man.
I have a filter and
I cannot easily get down to the core instincts.
I get into relationships where women hurt me.
This is because I am used to being hurt
From my adolescent rape.
I am identifying with my abuser.
And I need to get fucked.
And I need to psychologically help
The person fucking me.
I long for comfort by trying to cure a similar abuser.
The underlying instinct is complicated and abstract,
Each individual views the instinct itself
Through their own individually developed filter.
I do not have any male friends,
I thought this was because I preferred the company of
        Women.

I do not have male friends
Because I am scared of men because I am afraid of their
Penises.
I was hurt so badly by a penis.
And so time passes and my filter develops.
I need to learn
How to make a healthy relationship with a woman
        Who does not hurt me.
I need to make healthy relationships with men.
I do not need to
Save all the people with mental disorders.
My problems are easily listed
And I have come far in finding them
And finding out why I engage in
Self destructive behavior.
I just cannot even begin to
Find a solution to fix my filter.
My filter is fucked.
I am idling in neutral.

I cannot change the past, present, or the future.
How come I no longer have a choice whether
I go to the hospital at 16 or stay home?
What choice does George Washington have
About becoming the first president?
We make time seem important when in reality
Time has already left.
The present is gone with the action,
Action can be defined as movement or thought.
The action is done with a past premise.
The premise is always indicative
Of what one feels is the best mode of action
While the action is taking place.
It is tough to comprehend the reality
That our actions are controlled by our best try,
Even if it is not what we perceive as our best try
Then it is still the best we
Could have done at that given moment
And proven by the premise: we would not want
For bad.
Then without provocation the future
Churns away into the past.
I planned to write about something and here it is.
Now it is written.
It was the future now the past.

There is always only time;
The future is never controlled by our realizations
And appropriate responses.
The future is controlled by whatever animal instinct
Causes a certain action in time
During that one moment, which is already gone now.
There is no such thing as will power.
People created religion to solve free thought,
God gave us free thought: the greatest gift
        Then God made us
Or told us so much of what to do, or so the book goes.
What of God's divine plan?
Right and wrong?
Just action?
Our moral systems?
We all try our best even if we do not think so.
The only thing that separates
One person from another is individual capability.
We would believe that a successful person
Could overcome obstacles
Because of sheer will power.
But a successful person either obtains success by
Natural ability, like a sports star
Or by having a relentless perseverance
Like those people who overcome something bad
And make it good through a born inherent ability,
Or the lucky people.
They are powerful (or lucky) people from the start,
We would all love to believe
That the only reason why we are not rich and famous
Is because we are not achieving our full potential,
For one reason or another.
And likewise we would like to laud a person
Who overcomes adversity.
'Want' is a double edged sword,
People do not 'want' to become superstars because
They think they are happier
Doing whatever it is they are doing in their lives;
But in reality we all 'want' to be a superstar -
        Look at the television.
These people tried their best
And it was better than others' bests.

No matter how fucking hard most people try,
Which they are already doing,
They still will not amount to anything
Famously notable.
Everything is just so simple,
People all out with a unified objective to do their best
At what they determine their best is,
From serial killer to disease curer.
Each person is born capable of only so much,
The outside world has its influence
The person has his level of success,
No free will, the time we say is 'now'
        Is history.
One can work harder and harder working more and more
But a person who is 'fat' and 'lazy' is
Literally working just as hard.
A 'lazy' person would never admit
Not being able to obtain more because with
Admittance comes self-acceptance,
Acceptance that they cannot be a TV superstar
Or a noble prize winner.
Someday people will begin to accept that their best
Is awesome; and not being able to be
A superstar is great
Because anyone is capable of doing great things,
Whether it be
Volunteer work or mentoring or raising a child
Or achieving a sense of personal happiness.
Some people say
That they are happy with very little and this is true
But most of those same people believe
That they are capable of doing more.
You are, however only capable of what is already done
That is the passing of time. The day left yesterday.
I am sure that there are also people
Who do not need to hear this because they
        Already know it or are in denial.
I also want to make a note
That this idea of happiness through success, especially
Financial success is a
Predominantly western religious idea, an idea spawned
        By the three main western religions of
Israel, Christianity, and Islam.

I know of many other religions, where people strive to
Achieve inner peace through meditation
And put little or no value on material items.
The untrue thought -
That we can all do something great
Is the nectar of our human spirit.
You will never be anything,
Unless you stop wondering and see beauty in ordinary life
        The greatness of difference is the only true,
Great universal accomplishment.

Time slowly tears you apart
And drops you back to the earth.
The earth creates a mind capable of what is done
With a perception of the future.
What is done is always the best
In respect to your ability, your real life exposures,
        And luck.
I am trying my best just like the
Alcoholic who beats his kids, just like the hero.
Everyone wants to be better
And they are not because they cannot
Or because they are going to be better
But have not yet been lucky.
Becoming better is differently defined for everyone
        Better as by paper education
Or as by financial gain are equally hollow.
If you become better or
Naturally achieve something
From happiness then you are better.
Do not try to become better,
Just try to become happier.
Almost no one ever looks at this world
And their life and is satisfied
Herein lies the only real likeness we all share
Herein lies the key to understanding
The nature of people
Herein is the essence of the human necessity
For illusion, a survival instinct.
The most helpful statement that I can make is
'Try to be happy.'

Try to understand your instincts
And develop a filter around
Being kind to others as a bridge
To your own happiness
Be happy.[43]

Time moved me while I watched myself go,
This way and that;
Forward and backward.
Life can be great and I can move someone else
In a positive direction.
I can say something that changes someone's life.
I can write something that changes my own life.

The little I do at my best makes
Me fear for less fortunate souls;
Makes me confident in a trip to heaven
In a golden chair eating with Manson and his family.
I hope that I make the right decisions and that in my
Instinctual free fall that I fly by and/or
Land in happiness.
Everyone tries their best in the now
Which does not exist
Therefore the concept of trying does not exist
I am so fucking vague and unclear and
Probably wrong I scare even myself.
My logic is definitely not sound or even coherent
I suck at writing.
Just be happy to be with who you are.[44]

A secret for a better mind frame
Would be to first understand the illusion,
And then understand that you can abandon the illusion
Because the illusion draws us to develop the icons
And goals that are unobtainable.

---

[43] 11/15/02: While manic I often develop solutions to problems which I later disagree with; this is an example of that. However during the episode I was sure that I had the solution. [44] 11/15/02: This an example of when I took a break from obsessing. I chased a solution until I got so exhausted that I had to give up. After I gave up I felt like a failure because my intentions at the beginning of the obsession were so grandiose. In the next verse the reader can observe that I returned to my obsessive thoughts. As I have indicated obsession usually leads to repetition, an unfortunate reality for a manic individual and for the readers of this book. If I made this book less repetitive I would have made it less manic.

We need to understand that we are doing
The best with what we have
And that we are all growing,
Becoming better with time;
Even if this world seems to be becoming worse.
I may be becoming more depressed
And aggravated with everyone
But at the same time my ability to
Self-loath is becoming greater
I can articulate my hate in a way that is great.

This writing is too short
For me to allow myself to indulge in this topic.
And after I have edited
I see that I repeated myself several times
Hence rendering the poetic value nothing,
But hopefully one of
The 3 or 4 repeated expressions of the basic idea
Are clear and helped shine a passage
To a new or slightly different mode of thought.
Suffice to say I tried and now I only hope
That the abstract pieces can be fit together
And that many will be able to divert
Their mode of thought
Just a little to experience the complex
And radical ideas that I have presented.
Hopefully one person will gain insight, will understand
The heavy weight that non-conventional thoughts bear,
Feel the loss of control and like it or hate it,
Just experience it.
I apologize for my lack of ability to
Articulate this idea
In a way that would be more clear and concise.
I am a pussy, I am insecure,
I cannot follow the means to the end
I work so hard to create.[45]

---

[45] 11/15/02: I again get too tired to continue a mode of thought because I was thinking so intensely. I begin this verse calmly but my deep rooted frustrations prevail; I did not achieve a goal that I had obsessed over.

I do like my dog
Like us all
Trapped inside
Until death, only can we hope for enlightenment.[46]

I just got home ten minutes ago.
I had a blast at a great strip club.
I did what I do in strip clubs
Which is manipulate and this time, like most times,
I think that I won.
Once inside I waited and waited,
Like an animal stocking pray
      I had a wad of 600 dollars
(Of house money)
Folded in my front shirt pocket.
The bulge in my shirt pocket
Was designed to be more of a mind fuck to the girls
      Than the mind fuck I got from the girls
Putting their tits in my face.
The place smelled like fucked flesh covered
By scented soaps and perfumes.
There were three floors in this club
And lots of pretty girls.
I watched the girls slide their slender bodies
Up and down the poles
      While they watched my bulging
Front pocket.
I reeled while in the presence of their perfect,
Soft bodies
      I was a little drunk, I drank more;
Watching their bodies move like sex on stage
Everything was so fucking bright
And tangible, palpable, palatable.
I was still able to show patience
Turning down most girls for dances.
Then one came up to me
And I knew, some innate ability fired
I knew that I could wear her down and catch her.

---

[46] 11/15/02: I do not know what the hell I was writing about here; again, this book is open for the reader's interpretation. Perhaps someone reading this book has a better understanding of this entire episode than me. After all, I am biased and close to the problem.

81

I talked to her,
I asked about what she wanted to be
And I actively listened
        And she gave me her phone number.
First she gave me her phone number
Then she showed me her I.D.
        I wanted the I.D. because I know people lie.
I asked her questions about the I.D.
While she could not see it
        I needed to be sure.
I joked about stalking her,
She laughed and invited me to dinner next Tuesday.
Then she tried to refuse the money
But she deserved it by refusing it.
The lights went on and blinded me.
I had my friend drive me home.
I am tired now, I have to go to sleep.[47]

---

[47] 11/15/02: In this verse I was impulsive and grandiose. Impulsivity is a serious problem that bipolar people face both in the depressive and manic state. Impulsive behavior can result in murder or suicide or even both. When I was impulsive (like many others) I could not tell the difference between right and wrong, even if I tried. I made quick decisions because that was simply how my brain functioned; I felt like I had to make fast decisions. I made decisions that I often regretted or that caused me pain.

WEEK 3 OF JUNE 2002

PART I

Hopefully I am more than nothing
And something within these pages speaks.
For I know that in this book of many languages
No one will get it all.
But if you want, just make something up that fits
I have many words tattooed on me.
If someone tells me what it means and they are wrong
I tell them they are right because
This world belongs to you,
And your perception of art is always right.
Even if not congruent with the artist
Your thoughts are the right ones;
Not the general opinion just the sole person.

There is not enough emphasis on you
In this growing world.
Everything is made for what the masses want.
I want to make something for you.
There is no emphasis on the individual these days.
I want to change that,
Let thousands of bands be pop music.
Let everyone be the most beautiful person in the world
Because you are the most beautiful person in the world
You are unique and you have talents
You are, in a great way, greater than everyone else.
You are more beautiful, in fact,
You are the most beautiful
To one, probably to many.

I am happier right now than a minute ago
Because through my vision
And by my curious being,
A great form of expression is being realized
At least for me.
I think the way to see anything right
Is to see a lot at once
Which creates chaos,

Especially in regard to thoughts from the heart
This is truly a fantastic moment
Writing over forty thousand words
That make nearly no sense,
I do not know whether I am
Wonderful, horrible, or just a little fucked up
Whatever it is, I feel good doing it.
Now I have to get back to something
With some substance.[48]

I am a slave to happiness, righteousness, and sex
Which is to say that I am a slave to
The mass's conglomerate.
I was killed by manipulation, turned mutilation
Then I got resurrected by no one person
          Doomed by my inheritance
To commit suicide out of shame.
Now I continue to die and reincarnate
Until God grants me relief.
Jesus, may no more blasphemy proceed
God,
May the Holy Spirit once again embed
Itself into a person.
God watches us in the same manner
We watch celebrity boxing
I am with error.
Once begot always alone,
The water stands still
Let the unexpected tremor exude greatness.
Let passion rock my weary boat.[49]

You can never generalize
You can never think that you know someone
By the way they
          Look or act.
Once you decide not to prejudge
You begin to think that you know someone
For who they are and
Then they fuck your best friend.

---

[48] 11/15/02: During the last two verses I was in a state of euphoria. I was grandiose thinking I was teaching people how to feel as good as I felt. Although these thoughts functioned as a provoking factor to an elevated mood, usually ideas that led to an elevated mood only functioned as an antecedent once during the manic episode. [49] 11/15/02: I hoped that my increased energy would help me achieve some divine unforeseen goal.

When she spread her legs that was my happiest time
Though not my most glorious moment,
Understand?

I learned a lot from the people in front of me
More than what I learned in books.
People sit around thinking
Or thinking that they are thinking
But they are only hovering around a likeness,
Even the even handed, the successes
They are like lint stuck on lint
Teaching others a direction
That would have been found anyways.
Pushing forward a limping dog
To its bowl of food
Some are so good and strong that they can carry her.

I hate that which carries the tone
Of all three singers.
I hate that which carries
No tone.
I hate that which carries the tone
Of many singers.[50]

And here it is the moment at which the fold ends me.
The moment that some hoped for
Life or death, maybe a resurrection
After a poor decision.

You could say that I am grabbing at straws
But I am grabbing at my dick because I found a way
To get my slow modem to play a hardcore flick.
While I write this shit.
Then, as the guy starts grunting and masturbating
And she opens her mouth and closes her eyes
I cum with him and pretend
That there is an open mouthed girl
        Under my computer stand.
I will look at his cum on her and say
'What am I doing that is so fucking gross, not again.'

---

[50] 11/15/02: I wrote this because I wanted to make the reader hate me so that if I killed myself people would
not care as much. I wanted to be perceived as a monster. I often used this method as I felt that death was
imminent after completing this book.

I am just joking, I do not watch porn, none whatsoever.
I am, however, a wiz on the computer.
The internet is a wonderful resource
I find the lowest prices on car parts.
I use the internet to find out vital information
About potentially dangerous
Weather systems.
I also use the internet to find out about colleges
And housing opportunities.

I visited a famous emporium for the insane.
I hid under the bed while they came into the room.
I slept over, I tried to watch out for him.
I could not save him from the terrors.
That place is purgatory.
My friend (at the time) was being touched
By another sinner
And the demons told him that the abuser
Was working on it;
That the abuser was getting better.
What a pain for both to endure.
I could relate to my friend's trauma,
It can be terrible
To be touched when you want to be left alone.
He did not spend much time there
I eventually brought him back to earth.
He was gay but obviously this did not mean that
        Other men had the right to touch him.
I can, however, not help but wonder if it is different
To be touched inappropriately by a member of the
Gender which you are attracted to.
I think that it does not matter which gender it is
When you are touched and you want to be left alone.
He lamented and eventually
He deceived the evil spawns
To find freedom.

Seriously, that place is terrible.
You can read about it in a book that was written
        By an angry inmate
Or you can look it up on the internet.

You think
'Is there really a place that
Costs hundreds of thousands of dollars a year
To help the destitute, the down trodden
And the place is terrible?' Yes.
People get nearly raped and staff does nothing —-
But hold out a hand for money.
I swear that I said to them 'my parents will pay cash'
And my time for entrance changed from two months
To two weeks
Some of this is hearsay,
But some of this is my brief encounter
With a group home.
The horror of that place
In the middle of nowhere.
I speak now, if you are there
Call the police if someone touches you
Press charges.
The place is fucking stupid, corrupt
A person violently pushing a girl over
On his way into her room
And proceeded upon entry to expose himself
Using crude sexual innuendoes.
She told him to stop
But the incidences kept on occurring
She told staff but still it continued
That place is a fucked up money driven
Space
Space[51]

I stayed at the Pavilion at Mclean Hospital
Spent my 35 grand.
The place is money driven
Overpriced.
Turn a blind eye onto the poor
Rob the rich.
The director of the program
should have been reading me bed time stories
In my room.
I should at least have had a comfortable bed.
I fucked girls in there
And I hurt both genders of the patients.

---

[51] 11/15/02: Unfortunately, there are many mental health facilities, well-funded or otherwise, that do not provide good care for their patients.

I have gone far this year
Last year at this time I spent a lot of money
On a stripper in Vegas.
Fucked a billionaire's daughter in a mental institution
And got the 'love of my life's' name tattooed on me.
Now, this year I volunteered at a special needs school
And now I have a position at this school.
I provide a wide spectrum of help
To children ages 9-12 in a classroom environment.
I track the children's behaviors
And compare them to their goal behaviors.
Their goal behaviors are tracked
By a series of point systems
For which the child receives
One point for each goal they obtain
During a certain 45 minute block in a day.
All of the children's goals change
And become more difficult as the
Child becomes more psychologically adept.
A goal maybe 'keep hands in own space,'
If the child is able to achieve this goal
Then I would give them 1 point,
If the child failed to achieve this goal
I would put down a 0
And at the end of the day all the points get added up.
Each child can get a certain amount of points in a day
For example,
Mike may get 53 out of 55 points on Monday.
I later log all this information onto the computer,
Writing down how many points
Each child got everyday and how many time outs.
If you do not know what a time out is
You're a fucking idiot.
In addition to the daily computer logs
I must also do weekly logs
I have to give an overview of how each child did
On achieving two specific goals
These goals are more detailed
And the answers are in paragraph form.
These goals also change as the child develops.
There are 10 children in the classroom.
I do not play a passive role in the classroom,
I am trained in Therapeutic Crisis Intervention
      And I am authorized to implement holds.
I am usually involved in 1 or 2 full holds a week.

Often, however,
Children will show a failure to be safe with their body
But no propensity towards
Serious physical or property damage
In these cases I will simply
Hold the child's hand or hug them.
The key part, however, to my crisis training
Is to avert the crisis entirely.
Most crises are averted
Because of people in positions like mine
Intervene early and use strategies
Of behavioral management to de-escalate a situation.
Some de-escalating tactics would include
Active listening, prompts, and redirection,
Redirecting for example
Is if a child was tantruming
Because she could not ride her bike
And I said 'let's play a game of chess.'
That example is lame but nonetheless
It is an example of a de-escalation technique.
There are many de-escalation techniques
And I have had to use all of them.
I have probably,
Like most of the other staff,
Invented some of my own strategies.
In the classroom I help the children
Learn effective coping skills
For real life problems and
I teach the children better
Communication methods to use with staff,
        Peers, and family.
I am actively involved with the children's families
And with DSS and prospective
        Foster parents.
I really do love my job
And I know that I make a difference
As I watch each one of
The children grow in leaps and bounds.
Things change,
I do not dress so good any more
But I am happier helping children
Who violently attack me -
More happy than between the legs
Of one of the most famous strippers in the country.

I just wish I had someone to share it with.
Let me find a love to make me stop talking
Of such terrible things
That my thirst be quenched without others dehydrating.

Just let the day break, break
Let all these words, though piercing,
Miss your heart's lake.
Let ignorance in depth or at face value not destroy
Someone that you do not understand.
I am not my words.
My thoughts, dark and perverse as they may be
Are no more than explorations.[52]

I bought the supercharger.
I bought headers and exhaust and tires.
The total including tax and installation is 11 grand.
I gave the guy 6 grand in cash and my car.
Quick decisions lay the eggs of disaster in my soul.
I have not the total amount of money
I should not have a car that can go so fast.
A hundred MPH to hundred and thirty MPH
Faster than a fast car goes
      Thirty MPH to sixty MPH.
I will use it and it may kill me.
I will not earn the money
Lest my powers of manipulation prove
      More prevailing than I think.
I am wondering, working all week, making a difference.
On a leash, drunk every weekend night,
      Swimming, clubbing.
Pussy an inch from my face, close but so far away.[53]

I have a bad disease.
That makes me do things I regret
But there are some things that I will never do, ever.
My linear thinking falls away as summer heats up.

---

[52] 11/15/02: Sleeplessness is common during a manic episode as is lack of appetite. This verse was written about the former, I usually do not suffer the latter, at least not to the same degree. Sometimes the sleeplessness is the result of guilt over an impulsive decision or over grandiose thoughts but other times the sleeplessness can be the antecedent towards other manic behaviors. I discuss this concept further in the epilogue. [53] 11/15/ 02: I wrote this verse directly after coming home from a four hour trip to purchase parts to make my car go faster. Though I was impulsive I saw the impulsive behavior and was unable to correct it. My behavior was like a man impulsively sticking his hand into a fire and then complaining about the pain but expressing a desire to burn his entire body. I have heard many bipolar people express this horrible mind frame of losing control.

I think from one side to another, back again
        Then into another universe.
I read the writings on the wall and it says 'feel good'
        'Be creative.'
I have some good ideas.
Blood for fame and fortune,
Lighting in pictures and naked models.
I will either shoot like a rocket into space
        Or run out of fuel, fall and maybe die.
I am willing to take the chance for fame.

Pink Floyd is a great band for today's generation
And to prove my above point:
Roger Waters was a man affected
By what many people are affected
Waters was traumatized as much
As the average American.
His only difference
Is his ability to express himself
Clearly and articulately.
He lost his father,
His mother was overprotective,
His wife cheated on him
He built a wall around himself to protect himself
Filling in the spaces caused by traumas
With material objects.
Buying stuff seldomly works at fixing problems.
Waters made millions and was respected by millions
Yet he seems unhappy because of a life lacking.
Money is the worst attempt at curing trauma
And/or (possibly relating to) depression.
The worse people have life, the more they buy to fix it.
Money is nothing.
Money is something important
To people who are starving and living from day to day
        Make sure not to confuse the issue.
I think being rich is overrated
But I understand how important it is for
An individual to make enough money to survive.
However
You cannot buy life
Though you can create it
Both literally and figuratively.

Kelly thinks she is not special enough.
She does not want to be involved in anything
For the wrong reason.
I am talking to her at this moment,
I went to college with her
        For a semester.
She was my only friend when I was going to college.
She was my only friend when I had problems
During this last summer.
She is a good person so I have to keep my distance.
She is young and changing and I, old and set.
She is a an idiot.
I have nothing against her but she is just dumb
And that will make her entangled in nothing
For the rest of her life.
I am insecure but through familiarity,
Comfortable with it.
She thinks that she knows everything
But she is an idiot.
Shut the fuck up, you droning, 'know it all' bitch.[54]

Everything that I am writing is happening
While I am writing it
Some of the time I write about situations
That have already happened.
I very rarely lie about myself or situations I am in.
Sometimes I change some dates, situations, and names
But the situations as they appear
Throughout these memoirs
Create parallel emotions to those evoked
By the original - 100% true to life situations.
I have not changed very much at all.
I was on the phone talking to that girl, I really was.
Right now I do not think she is
A bad person or dumb but I want to be honest
        To the moment.
I am thinking about what is happening
And so I write the thought as it comes.
My last writing was written
All while I was on the phone.

---

[54] 11/15/02: My impulsive mind makes me suddenly change my perception of a good friend over the course of two lines. Kelly said something and I hated her; when I am not manic I do not make such poor decisions. This was the last time I ever talked to her and she had helped me for two years and always had been a good friend. So many bipolar people tell so many different stories about how a manic episode ruined a good relationship. I do not show much guilt while manic which is an obvious problem.

Sometimes things are simple and sometimes
The depth of my idea is great.
Sometimes my intentions are
Good and I reread a passage and I think
'This writing really sucks,
It is at a middle school level, no one will get it[55]

The burden of being upright:
This society is fucked
Our society is based on rituals developed
By humans before
We learned enough about our spirit to understand one
Of the most important aspects
Of being humans is being able to
Develop compassion.
Society is based on negative reinforcement.
You are bad therefore you are punished
We so blindly accept a stupid premise
To believe and base a society on a broken book
Written over 2000 years ago.
As people we have grown so far psychologically
And yet we are drawn to answers from a book where
We can learn how to fuck, how to discipline,
       How to make slaves.
Punishment is most often induced
By someone committing an indistinguishable crime
Like Aaron, Moses' brother who is
Faithful and loves God.
Aaron makes some minor mistake that offends God.
Moses brings him atop some mountain
In front of all the Israelites
Makes him strip naked, gives his clothes to his son
Then God strikes down Aaron.
(I think that this execution
Has something to do with Egyptian or Greek influence
The infamous golden cow,
That Aaron worshiped stands as a god figure in
Both Greek and Roman myth and Egyptian culture.
The ironic part is that
God's ability to strike down with lightning
Is an idea created by the pre-Hellenic religions,

---

[55] 11/15/02: One should note that I have changed this text more (upon legal advice) after I stated my changes
in this verse.

Zeus, cloud gatherer,
He is the only god I know who uses lighting
Or maybe Zeus's father Cronus,
Or Cronus's father Uranus, all used lightning
All existed well before the Bible began,
according to me.)
One would think
That we have learned something since then
I commit a crime, put me in a jail,
Let me be sodimized, let me be punished
Like in Sodom when Lot's wife
Turned around and was turned to salt
Then Lot's daughters got him drunk
To fuck and continue the line.
No one deserves that.
It is a silly story which is one of many that comprises
        The book which we base our lives on.
You have to be fucking retarded not to get it,
Read Leviticus on the Sanctity of Sex
This passage of the bible specifically states
'you will not lie with a man in the manner in
Which you lie with a woman.'
You have to be an idiot not to get it,
There is no strange interpretation that would make
These statements not mean the obvious.
Find a new fucking God
        If this one exists.
He hates you. I would hate Him if I believed in Him.
Let me be beaten and punished for someone else's mistake
I have a responsibility to help those who cannot
Help themselves
A criminal cannot help his or her actions.
Every crime is my fault,
I knew right but could not make him or her
Implement a more productive action in leave of a crime.
The premise of jail is to separate a prisoner
From society until rehabilitated
But that is bullshit.
I wake up all the time thinking
'I am going to shoot this guy in the fucking head,'
Then I think 'fuck I forgot that I would get arrested,'
So then
        I go back to my everyday life.

No criminal commits a crime because they want to
And the few that do are so mentally unfit for society
That they should
        Have been aborted,
They should have been recognized earlier.
We will never be able to recognize
The next Manson or local drug dealer
Because they rot unstudied in jail or are executed.
We have no recourse because we do not understand them
Because we are in part afraid and in part not allowed.
This country over-estimates how many people think
They can get away with a crime,
In retrospect to how many people live in poverty
And how many people are mentally disturbed.
It is infinitely more comfortable
To believe criminals make choices than to accept
That there are people walking around who need our help
And only we (the sane) can help them from hurting us.
We are scared to think that we need to do more,
'With power comes responsibility.'
We do not want that power,
It would be too much of a burden.
All killers are seriously mentally disturbed.
I cannot imagine the mental backlash
I would get from killing
I would probably kill myself.
Normal people,
That is people who are sane and
Have the monetary means necessary to
Support life, do not commit serious crimes.
People who commit murder should go to a psychologist
Find the root of the problem,
Try to rehabilitate or at least
Try to learn how to detect future violent criminals.
We could learn how to find out what is wrong
And implement strategies to deter criminals
        From either starting a life of crime
Or stopping a criminal from another crime.
Anyone who would commit any crime needs help,
Not punishment.
The bible will say blood for blood, eye for an eye.
The bible has the ten commandments,
'Thou shalt not kill,'
Yeah we should not kill but then God
States His reasons to kill.

I can kill in God's name,
According to the Bible
Someone should stone me to death
For fighting with my parents.
That is bullshit;
It defeats the purpose of conscious thought,
People think that they are rational beings
Because they can reason
But all people have reasoned
Is that it is okay to act like animals.
To be killing in the name of God
And other lesser digressions.
A group of my peers
On a panel called a jury condemned me to murder
Now since a doctor cannot kill me,
Someone else will have to follow the order,
I will have to have someone
Without medical knowledge murder me.
I was just murdered by a jury,
I do not understand how people can bear the burden
Of being able to have
Absolute judgment over another's life.
Truly, what should separate us from animals
Is that we do not need negative reinforcements.
A dog does, the dog shits on the floor
You push its face in it
The dog remembers that and discontinues the action
That earned the punishment.
People should not be punished,
Punishment is an unnecessary effort and pain for
The civilized being, we must only correctly punish
Our young to encourage free thought.
Children learn right from wrong
Through positive redirection and consequences
Later they form their own ideas
Which serve as their standard for conduct
Once the child learns
He or she no longer needs punishment
Because they learned
        How to rationalize,
In a given situation, the right and wrong approach.
Then they have become an adult
And if they digress they have a better chance
At rehabilitation because
They have some basic understanding of morals.

But adults need more explanation and correction
In order not to do something wrong.
Most violent adults are born in a violent family
        Violence is born and raised
Violence is rarely innate.
If the problem is innate
Then early warning signs should be observed
And the child should receive proper
Medication and therapy
In order to live the life that he/she deserves.
We can and are able to reason with one another
Yet most states still commit murder
A jury kills hundreds of Americans every year,
It is retarded
Most of us are not retarded.
We kill children every year,
The only other places
That do that are some third world
        Countries, such as Iraq.
Very few doctors are going to try to stop violent
Criminals because
Sitting down and doing therapy sessions
With violent criminals can be scary.
There is a lot of pressure on someone
Who is treating a criminal because if the criminal
Has a relapse,
The relapse may be in the form of a murder.
In jail if someone is released and commits murder,
The prison has no burden.
The prison was obligated to punish, not to save,
Making things easy in the short run
Does not always pan out in the long run.
Growing prisons, growing crime rates.
The only reasons I think of for why some crime
Has gone down is early intervention,
And more job opportunities,
        Not prison.
Adults do not respond to threats;
They respond to psychology and rationalization.
A criminal's rationale behind a crime supercedes
That of the idea of potential punishment
Much like how most of us speed,
The idea of speeding slightly
(5-10 miles over the speed limit)

We rationally perceive the relevant danger
Of speeding and
Speed anyways
Because we do what we feel is right despite the law.
What we choose to do almost always supercedes
The idea that we may be punished
Because the punishment would be unjust.
Justice is personal.
Each person believes in their own standard of justice,
Not the one imposed by the government,
That was taken from the bible,
Each person perceives their action
As just and appropriate.
All people are just.
One person may feel
Justice can be achieved while stealing
Because he/she justifies the action
Because he/she is feeding a family
Or one might feel that it is owed to them.
The criminal system is fucked
It is based on a premise of dead ideas,
Killed by our growing,
Developing minds,
I would be wrong to write all this
Without a proposal for expenditure;
It would cost millions for prisons
To change into mental institutions.
I propose that if someone is helped
In a mental institution
That he/she will not only recover much faster
But he/she will also not commit another crime
This will already save more than the cost
Of staff therapists.
I also believe in a different type of police
With a different type of training.
I believe that money should be taken from
Too many policemen
          Using too many high tech. gadgets
And that money should be given to early aid
Such as early education,
I believe that the police force
Should be smaller and better trained
With less emphasis on problems
Like minor teenage recklessness
And more emphasis/money

On children getting better educations
More money should be spent on
Drug prevention and education than spent on
The operations to intercept drugs and
On jail cells for people who need something else.
People need to be taught how to rationalize properly.
Proper rationalization can be simply
Described as the qualities of one
Who does not seriously, emotionally or physically,
Hurt others, and whose concepts
Of reality are similar to the majority of his/her peers.
A person should also be taught it is okay
To be happy with their lives.
I think that people need to be taught this
From a young age
And these ideas should be reinforced throughout life.[56]

All people deserve to be happy.
If an individual decides that his view of happiness is
Being fucked up the ass
While five people pour pudding over his head,
That's cool;
As long as no one is getting hurt and as long as all
The people engaging in the activity are of a mature age.
And here it comes:
I think that when a person reaches
The age of fourteen that they should be granted
        Total, unlimited freedom.
At fourteen you are really free anyways,
Why should you not be allowed
        To do what you want.
You have access to drugs and alcohol,
Cigarettes and you can fuck.
You can kill yourself.
People own their body,
The government does not own you
Nor does your doctor or your parents.

---

[56] 11/15/02: I would not have been able to write a passage like this if I had not been manic. My mania resulted in me staying up all night reading books and writing. I had an infinite amount of energy driven by every type of conceivable emotion. Almost all the manic or hypo manic people I know are tremendously productive. I believe that not only was I manic in this passage, but also through the entire book.

You are going to do what you are going to do
        I just think that you should be heard
And be a part of the world
A part of the voting system, able to change the world
Able to follow your own heart.

It is your choice to live.
If death seems eminent
Because of depression then take it
You will sit in heaven.
Everyone is loved by God and everyone is going somewhere.
Just be happy, do not stress about what others think.
Leave your husband if he makes you miserable
Become a coke-head porn star
Or become the first female president
But do not base your decision on
        Religion, politics, and society.
Let your lifestyle decisions be based on
Your own rationalization.
One must be self-reliant in decision making
Or else you are making someone else's decision.
You can only be happy if you can
Make decisions for yourself
Because only you know exactly what you want.
I believe if each of us is being true to ourselves
The world will be a more beautiful place
For more colors will blindly be heard
Through clarion horns.
Most people will choose a productive lifestyle because
Who wants to be a stoned porn star
If you think about it and the STDs and
The unfulfilling relationships
The job is unattractive.
When you examine the prospect
Of heavily using drugs, you understand
How they destroy your being
And how they destroy the lives of those you love.
You will decide not to use drugs.
There will be the few,
But the many should help them,
And the many will just be a little more free,
I truly believe in ultimate capitalism in anarchy.

PART II

I have no more money
And all I can think about is these abstract ideals.
I have so many relevant issues
In my life that get skirted.
I tripped and fell somewhere on a tropical island and
        When I woke up I was lying in my bed.
I was chasing something
I lost everything, I owe so many so much money.
My body drives me back into the smoke-filled rooms
The floor shakes from the bass
While girls elevate their emotional state;
Playing games using precision
And calculation designed to hurt,
They are so fucking cool.
I sit in the corner with dead eyes,
Watering from stale smoke.
Cheap perfume draws my attention,
Cheap cologne makes my mind run.
And all I can think about is
Emily or religion or becoming famous.
The book.
I am numbed, the people move slowly then I stand up.
People speed up as soon as I approach,
From slow motion to blurring speeds.
        I cannot keep up.
My mouth is dry, I buy another beer,
I talk to another girl
Who walks away,
I do not think that she could even hear me.
I get drunk, I yell, I get kicked out,
I piss in the parking lot, I fight and bleed.
Late night breakfast and quick words,
Still I remain silent
Everyone in slow motion until I speak.
I am going out tomorrow night too,
Because my cruel replacement
For Emily lurks in the basement of a night club.
Decked out in expensive clothes, pretty,
And under-aged.
She has a black heart, and I will find her.
Just like my abuser found me.
Without that pain,

I am only a fly.
I cannot feel unless it is pain,
Find me someone to inflict that pain, someone
     That I can fuck
Show her off to the world.
To continue down this road is to be re-traumatized.
I am too scared to proceed walking in this direction.
I need to walk somewhere else.
I need to feel like I am writing something
As relevant to you as
To me.[57]

God stands up in heaven looking down on a sinner,
Who lived bad up to twenty five,
Then turned his life around and became
A priest who helped many.
That same man could get hit
In the head by a rock at 23 and die,
And go to hell or purgatory and suffer
That is fucked.
God does exist;
The science behind the luck of life prevailing proves it,
Despite Nietzsche's 'God is dead,' God is alive again;
Just because we disproved one god or two or 200,
Does not mean that there is not a God.
We exist to propel ourselves beyond God.
Like any parent God would like to see us
Become greater than what he/she/it/they
Is/are/was/were.
Maybe God/gods is/are dead and
Now we must do better if only because
We are capable, if only to survive
As a species or to bring something good
To this cold, dark universe.
There are no boundaries to the good that
Humankind can do.

---

[57] 11/16/02: This was a psychotic state that I was in where not only my perception of reality was altered, but also my actual vision. I have heard many people explain having been psychotic in a similar manner while manic; these people, like myself, were able to function normally for a long period of time despite these psychotic episodes.

People can create life and make it great.
One day we will grow fantastic,
It is in our nature.[58]

I think a lot about that girl, Emily.
She told me she was a Dido.
But she was really pregnant by a bull
With a Minotaur in her womb.

My Emily the succubus.

I am starving,
Out of boredom.
I can run,
But my legs hurt because I worked out.
I worked out because
I wanted to become more attractive.
The rhythm plays loud within my aching head,
Aching because I cannot stop to think why.
She will never find me because I left.
I left because I am a bad person.

Nothing I read does more than evoke an emotion
Drawing from the knowledge I have already earned.
That is not true,
I have learned new information from books.
I find, however,
That a good book does not give me an idea,
A good book simply stimulates an emotion.
Right now that precious emotion is anger and depression.

I cannot dance.
Nor can I sing or play an instrument.
I do not know if my art is His grandchild.
Maybe my art is a bastard grandchild.

---

[58] 11/16/02: I have once again returned to one of my many obsessive thoughts. It is noteworthy to say that I become more and more repetitive the longer I have the episode. Almost all the people I know who are bipolar suffer their symptoms worse and worse until medicated or until experiencing a catastrophe. Many doctors believe that bipolar is a degenerative disorder where in some cases people go psychotic from an episode and become schizophrenic and bipolar for the rest of their lives. Schizophrenia according to the Merriam Webster dictionary is 'a psychotic disorder characterized by loss of contact with the environment, by noticeable deterioration in the level of functioning in everyday life, and by disintegration of personality expressed as disorder of feeling, thought (as in hallucinations and delusions), and conduct.' I think that most people with schizophrenia and doctors would agree with this definition though it is very condensed; people should consult the national foundation of mental health, a psychiatrist, or a person suffering from the disorder for more information.

I am going to stop writing.
I am going back to college to get my business degree,
Then I am going to take over my father's business,
And many a trophy wife,
Who only loves me for what I do for her.
She will cheat on me all the time and I will know it
Only not admit it to myself.
I will occasionally cheat on her.
Then we will have a child
The child will not bear my blood,
And I will treat both my daughter and son
In the same manner.
The most lascivious woman is a rich man's wife.
She finds the nothing that money is and cheats
With the something that someone else
Emotionally possesses.
I will name my child Bastard Feldman.
And little Bastard will grow up and
Take over the company.
Everyone will think my wife, my child, and I are fine.
Me, my wife, little Bastard who will have
Bastard Jr. then Bastard the II,
Because Bastards will keep the legacy alive.
My child will be able to take name
Because Bastard will also take her Christianity,
My God does not allow me to name my child after myself.
And Shane is a bad name anyways.
Bastard will become less and less
Capable with time because the line
        Will become deluded.
Each father and son will be unrelated.
Had my child been mine,
His blood would promise his fortune.
So now, instead,
We have a million tainted-blooded, spoiled rich idiots.

Girls are so loud during sex.
Do you know why?
It is because men had to spend so much time
Learning how to jerk off quietly.
That son of a bitch God that exists
Abandoned us, I wonder who God fucked to get us?
And so bad we were that God left.
And in our parents absence we created a God,
We created many different parental icons.

104

God is simply our Father
In accordance to popular western religions.
We even call priests father.
Who is Mom? The earth.
God stuck his dick in the dirt,
Moved it around until he ejaculated;
Then when Mother Earth got pregnant, he skipped town;
Went back to heaven to live the good life.
While Dad lives the bachelor's life,
We all beat up on our abandoned mom,
Asking her for all kinds of stuff,
While Father says, "What? I do lots of stuff"
Dad says, "I perform miracles and other stuff,"
Mother rolls her eyes at him.
But God is truly taking advantage of the situation,
We cannot handle the truth
That God is up in heaven
Fucking one of our pretty daughters who ascended,
God is probably making his most righteous
Beautiful daughter dessert, He is all powerful.
Earth is a good parent but like all parents
(Especially single parents) she is having
Problems and she has her own personal needs.
She should ask dad for child support.
Take dad to family court.
I can see the episode on 'Divorce Court.'
The judge will make
Mom take a DNA test.
The test will show that Dad is not really Dad,
And Mother will say, "there was someone else"
While shaking her head.
And next we will end up on 'Jerry Springer,'
Mother Earth with God and Jesus.
Jerry will say to God,
"We have someone backstage
I think you would like to meet,"
The crowd will ohhh and awwww
Then from behind the stage another man will come out,
And the real father will not be accepted,
The violent implosion will take a seat,
And we will only call him by his first name,
The 'Big Bang.'
And that name 'Big Bang' will be so appropriate
Because that is what he did to Mom;
Then Dad will hit Big Bang

And Jesus will start trying to mediate.
Then just like on every other fucking episode
Of the Jerry Springer Show,
The only person in the crowd more dysfunctional
Than the guests will get up,
She will say, "Who is the person in the robe, again?"
And Jerry will say, "Jesus"
And she will take the mike back and say,
"All I have to say is, Jesus,
And all of God's creations why are you stay'in with your
Mom, you know you need to get a real job
And be on your own."
And we will make up lies
To cover up the fact that we do not have the means
To move out of Mom's place
And go somewhere that is all our own, that we built.
We will say that we are helping Mom and
That our presence is crucial
But in reality we are speeding up her demise.
Jesus will start to cry and say,
"Mom how could you do this."
I think that is where the story stops
This is where society is now
In respect to Mom and Dad and our real father.
We are still running DNA tests
On Bang to be totally clear.
There is more but I am sleepy
So I will leave it for another book on another day,
Sweet dreams.[59]

The pole rusted, cracked, then hit the floor,
And I don't care because I hate jumping;
I do not suck at jumping
But I get tense in front of all these people.
        I screw up under pressure,
Or at least I think I do.
I will just continue to write shit,
Because that is an inherent key toward my objective
Of a prompt finish.

---

[59] 11/16/02: The reader should note that in an effort to speed up the text, so that my racing thoughts are better represented, there are going to be less footnotes; thus, letting the reader relate to my fast-paced life. I have already described most of what is going on; as the book progresses I suffer from most of the same problems, however they are becoming more acute.

The wind caresses my finger tips
As I see the only infinity,
And while the sun is sinking
And the water turns a deep blue,
My thoughts regress,
My face expressionless peers deeper into the water.
I am positive that I will find something further.
The tide hits like rain drops and my damaged soul sighs.
The smell of salt brings tear drops from
Yawning memories.
Now the sound of the tide exaggerates
The shine of the moon
And the other lesser lights in the sky.
The laminated world is frozen
And congealing into a single emotion.
I feel good while without.
The beauty of the moon,
The smell of the ocean, and the feel of sand.[60]

I am tired of the rants and complaints,
Alone he is the foundation of something
Without that pretty voice and the back up band,
So alone, it is beautiful.
Like a single tree surrounded by a river
Of dead sand in a desert.
So it is naked, and everything naked
Has beauty and ugliness.
I care not about how pretty the skin
But for the uglier soul, which
Defeats my personal control
And leaves my lecherous desires.
Maybe only leaving my lust
My lust will naturally, admittedly, not knowingly,
Follow my fall
But money is worse,
Having the propensity to make me manipulate,
I have the means to make the most
Insidious reptile come forth
The lust, the money,
Give way to the chase of soft skin, pretty face.
Rough outside inside soft-like pussy lips.
I never even found you, I only saw you once in passing.

---

[60] 11/16/02: I was writing a lot about beautiful imagery in an effort to escape reality; sometimes when I wrote about reality I got tremendously distraught.

To be the closest and furthest away and the first.
I hope that your cuts still shine purple,
Like a crayon in heat.
I hope you fuck well, like a rock star.
I hope you are still your beautiful self.
From fifteen to twenty-one.
The last 7 lines are for Jordan.
The seven before are for my future.
9 and 7 and 8 and 9 and 0
And 2 and 1 and 1 and 0 and 1.
I'm fucked and the appeal stops
After the drugs stop or start wearing off.
I am a teenager, fifteen maybe. Maybe 16
My fans will not exist because my nothingness
Became palatable from my sucking
I now taste like my wet kisses.
I am a loser because my personality
Is volatile.
I mean that.
Perhaps, I will kill myself
And affect those people around me that care,
I have descended away, I am Virgil,
Doomed to take you through Dis.
My only difference is Virgil wrote a good book.
In actuality I will probably be a male version
Beatrice shuttling you off to heaven
Like a baggage boy explaining the splendors
Of your hotel room while carrying
Up your bags.
I read the bible everyday for 15 minutes and I pray.
The bible told me I can do what I please
As long as I follow God's will.
I like Martin Luther more than the Pope;
I do not need a middle man.
I can, however, manipulate what the bible means to me,
Hell, look what Europeans did during the
Crusades and the Muslims: the Arabs.
We are in the age of manipulation,
'It depends on what your definition of is, is.'
I could function in accordance to Jesus and Moses,
But I already disgraced them.
I am going to do what I deem righteous
Because I have seen so many people
Do so many terrible deeds following the
Directions that they thought were God's word.

I am no member of the Manson family.
Look at Charles Millis (Willis) Manson:
Listened to the Beatles and sang folk music,
Read the bible
Charlie even studied Scientology.
But he did develop a methodical plan to create
A race war
And he did order the savage murders
Of more than 10 people.
I do not believe that Charlie's Will Is Man's Son,
I do not understand
'Killing in the name of your God/gods "name here."'
I do not believe that Charlie was a prophet.
But my own examples give way to my self-doubts
So just in case:
I have the real Jesus in my heart
And these words are simply printed on this page,
Heaven's door will still be ajar
When it is time for reckoning.
In reality I will probably hang around
And get married, grow old, and die.
Live a good Christian life.[61]

I swear that I just get worse and worse
My poetry and prose are just fucking terrible now.
Am I here or there?
Is this good or bad?
Or corny?
Or does my wild style make sense, awkwardly beautiful?
My naked body is on display for anyone to stop and look.

And next I will write something normal.
I am tired of complaining and fixating on God.
I am going nuts.
I will write something normal.

(Ironically, today, one day after the above 4 lines were written I visited Emily
and after engaging in unprotected intercourse she reveled that she had used an
unclean needle for the use of heroine. Now I am going to write about how I feel
pertaining to how she treated me this evening directly addressing the possibility
that I might have contracted AIDS or another serious disease.)

---

[61] 11/16/02: This verse has a similar content as do verses in earlier weeks, however, in this verse my ideas are
becoming more real. In this verse and in the verses to come I may be obsessive and repetitive (at times) but I
was becoming more and more consumed by my behaviors.

Emily, you fucking whore.
I wanted to write something interesting
But you just ruined it by pissing me off.
How could you fuck me after you used a shared needle.
You probably just fucking gave me a disease of death.
It serves my complaints well.
I knew you were bad but I trusted
You when we had sex unprotected,
       I thought you would warn me.
I have never been so pissed off and felt
So much poetic irony at the same time.
I cannot believe I even came over to your fucked house,
       For you to prove your poisonous ways,
(Maybe the above is still correct).
You fucking cunt, whore, bitch.
You fucking lying, ugly whore.
You God-damned succubus
I can see you with my eyes closed,
Bright red blood on your lips
Dripping down off your chin
From a thousand men's blood drained hearts,
Two needles stuck in your head
As horns filled with product.
In reality
Your face is fucked
By sand passing through the narrow.
You look older and have lost your soft appearance.
Your body has become heavy in different areas.
Your body has changed from a limber,
Tight teenager to an adult.
Not all adults are ugly,
A lot are pretty but a lot of
Pretty young girls make bad adults.
Remember Kim when you met her,
You whore, two more years until you are gone.
Your adult body is going to be all distorted and ugly.
You are disproportioned;
Each part of your body does not compare
Properly to the other.
You are a ruby thrown against a rock.
Your breasts have nipples too big
For the amount of cleavage you have.
Your tits are so ugly and misshapen.
Your body and face are tattered
And ruined beyond recovery.

Sure any guy will still fuck you
But no one will stay with you.
They'll use you for money.
You malice screwed up backward ugly
Whore of a fucking beast.
Every time that I pulled my dick out,
The stench of your rotten pussy disgusted me
In a way that made sex seem not even worth it.
I wanted to leave you the whole time,
I was held by your money and the suicide threats
You would make about killing yourself if I left.
I tried and I tried and I tried
And I tried and I tried to break up with you
I should have let you overdose on heroin and die,
Self-centered bitch.
I swear to God that everything I write is the truth
I did not embellish or exaggerate, I always hated you
And now I finally have an outlet.
I am not writing out of anger,
I have looked again and again at your snake-ridden head
Hell found me worse on earth you
Wicked, smelly, whore, fucking druggy cunt.
I only went once with you because twice
Would have been repelling.
Your pussy smelt as the most foul fish,
One would beg death to escape the rapture,
Seriously, you cannot do
Anything about that abomination of a pussy.
Your stench is a sin against God.
I was bored and I hated you,
I hated everything about you.
I told my parents from the start,
My mom, dad, and my sisters.
I thought you were ugly with an even uglier soul.
My mother whom you think loves you
So much always thought you were phony
        And rightly so.
My sisters felt disdain towards you
Because I told them a lot of your wicked ways.
When I first met you
I told my parents I thought you were
My personal anti-Christ
And I only stayed with you because you let me
Cum inside you and sodomize you.

I told everyone that I was using you,
I told everyone I was ass-fucking an 18 year old.
Fuck you!
I hope you fucking try to look again
As you did when I met you
No matter how skinny you get you will be ugly.
Fucking uneducated cunt, dirty,
Fucking manipulative whore.
I told all my friends I hated you
And all my friends thought you were an Amazon
Not solely because of height;
They thought you were manly and told me to run.
Everyone told me the money was not worth it.
Whore, liar!
Smelly cunted whore, swimming in sin,
You lecherous demon woman!
I told everyone how you were crazy
And would threaten to overdose on heroin or cocaine
Only to get your way.
I told them how you treated everyone like shit
And you thought you were a princess.
I hated you with that Britney Spears pop attitude,
And now you are old, ugly, and dilapidated.
Now for the mental:
Kill yourself and do the world a favor.
No one in your family is crazy,
They never did anything to you.
You just pulled temper tantrums every time
You did not get exactly what you wanted.
Your mother and father are fine,
You were just fucked from birth,
Destined to be a cold-hearted selfish bitch.
Everyone around you knows you have these qualities
They just do not want to hurt you.
People either want to fuck and leave,
Take your money, or both.
You are spoiled rotten.
You do not nor will you ever understand
What it is like to need.
You will never live.
Even the worst person would be too good for you.
You manipulate your stories pertaining to the past,
Consistently modifying important
Details to mask the fact that you
Hurt everyone who came near you.

The truth being: you hurt them more than they hurt you.
Nothing has ever gone wrong in your life
And you are given everything
And all you do is bitch and whine;
The only cure for you is to overdose.
Everyone is going to treat you like shit
Because you are a shit stain on society.
You are only concerned about yourself
And what you want.
You are a piece of shit.
You steal massive amounts of your parents' money
For nothing.
You have the coldest heart I have ever seen
And the actions you receive from others
Will always be a mirror of your cruel ways;
So expect to be treated like shit, marry a shallow trophy
Who really hates you but is fun to fuck and
Will fuck you over.
You probably won't even find someone fun to fuck
You will have to settle for some sleaze ball
Who treats you like shit
Because you cannot do any better
Than an asshole boyfriend
And you deserve an asshole boyfriend.
You are going to get a disease,
You are going to become smellier and dirtier still.
You are unlovable, you do not have one redeeming quality,
You are mean, you lie,
You take advantage of other people, you rage at nothing.
You are a crazy, lying, ugly, manly whore.
No one will ever love you because you are an asshole.
Look what you did to me,
I have been loyal to you since I met you.
I wish you were here.
All you told me about was how you loved me.
Lying daughter of Satan, Queen Whore.
You voluntarily swore to God a million times over
How you could not live without me,
How you would always find me and make sure
That we were together.
You cheated on me while we were together,
Twice letting one of them cum inside you,
Then after we talked about making a life commitment
You fucking hooked up with
Another fucking dirty dickhead.

I had to make a fucking doctor's appointment
Every three months to make sure I was
        Not infected by your whorish ways.
I cannot blame you because your
Soul already descended to hell, fucked by a penis fatter
Than your head, while everyone you trusted
Eats your flesh.
You ate my dignity.
The true you is already frozen
And the demon now holds your earthly body.
That is your Hell - study your fucking books better.
It is your religion.
Go back to fucking school,
From education you would understand your terrible ways.
I thought I was dying of a brain tumor
And that I would have to put my dog to sleep
And when I called I could not reach you,
I could not reach you because
You were spending all your time with a fucking dealer,
With whom you fucked a day after we separated,
I thought I was going to die,
Not to mention your promise to an everlasting
Relationship.
You committed the worst sin,
Betrayal and murder of the souls of those who loved
You. Strangers do not feed her scarlet poisoned belly,
Fill her black womb.
If you have a baby it will be more fucked than you,
Your baby's soul will be
Alongside yours in hell everlasting.
All I wanted was someone to talk to.
What kind of a cold-hearted bitch does that,
You stinky twatted sadistic whore.
Then after the great effort I took to forgive and
The day before I had to go back to work
You had me come over your house like
You were having an emergency.
Then we had sex only for me to find out
That you had used a dirty needle
        Less than a month ago.
I could have a fucking STD,
Fucking mutation of a soul schism.
You swore to me,
You wrote me love poems, you said
        I made you happy.

You said I was the only one to make you happy.
How could you swear to me so much
And then betray me, may you rot,
May you suffer a most terrible life
And die a cold lonely bitch.
You swore to me for five months, I got you out of Hell.
I kept you from overdosing,
I guess I should join that fucking club.
You fucking wreck!
I was always there for you and I never
Asked for anything back.
Think long and hard about our relationship
I never asked you for a fucking thing, God is my witness.
God the creator,
The wisdom brought by Jesus,
And the love born to the Holy Ghost
You methodical, manipulating cold-hearted bitch,
Who violated His Ghost
And His Power, you let Him die in vain.
You Hell spawned whore.
You desecrated everything holy and everything good.
You swore to me for three months,
Now you have sworn to God a million times,
Condemning you to a million times
Eternity in that harsh hell
You have received eternal damnation.
Repentances are useless on a sin of this magnitude.
Trust me, a priest may say to save you
But he would only speak without the knowledge of
        The great depth of your ocean of sin.
A priest to save you could not because
He could not know you,
Maybe you can get one to fuck you,
Prove the greatness of your faith.
Worst of all you betrayed me
And as your eternal lover you betrayed your family.
Betrayal of family makes you the worst,
Most fucked up terrible whore.
You have abandoned your God.
You were not a sixteen year old promising
A high school sweetheart the world.
You were eighteen, you were an adult.
You will destroy anyone around you,
Both your family and Adam are examples of people
        Made crazy from you, stressed out by you.

Everyone knows that you are a phony,
I took you to exotic romantic places.
What did you do for me, name one fucking thing?
Name one thing that is not corrupted
By you stealing money from your parents
       I.E. the gold bracelet?
You went shopping and then came
Short for cash for my bracelet?
I should thank your fucking dad
For what he bought me, you had no right to steal from
Your family, you betrayed them
And it was because you could not stop shopping
For even a second even to save enough
To buy me something nice.
So I had to give you a loan to buy me my gift
Which you later repaid me with
       An unauthorized check from your parents.
You spent the loan on yourself.
You selfish web-footed freak.
Sex sucked, I like to fuck all night,
But your rank polluted pussy prevented that.
You are not tight, except in your asshole,
Which is still comparatively loose,
Name one time when you have been there for me
When I have been emotionally downtrodden?
You lying dyke.
You are simply a bad person,
The extent of your existence is to bring pain to others
       You have never had someone hurt you.
Your only greatness is found in your ability
To inflict dilapidating or deadly emotional pain,
While you yourself somehow avoid any type of betrayal
Or other emotional hurt.
You bitch about nothing,
Every time after you would whine to my mom or family
       About how no one loved you;
They would say that you were a spoiled brat
Who tantrums to get what she wants.
Go burn a hole into your face,
Represent your void, stop the small stuff
The time has come to think big,
Look at those wrists get the razor.
You are also one of the most stupid people
I have ever met, you already know that.
You know you're a fucking moron.

You have no education,
You do not know anything about anything.
You are a stupid whore,
Who lies and betrays those who try to help.
Your fat ass looks like shit,
It falls low and does not give the appearance of
Two cheeks
You seem to have one ugly sagging
Piece of fat for a back.
No one likes you and no one will.
You will end up in Hell with shit on your face
Or more likely frozen somewhere
Being tortured by yourself for eternity, frozen.
You have no sophistication, no class.
You are a cruel person,
I still have those bullshit Valentine day cards.
You said that you would make it work,
No matter what, and you did not even try.
God will punish you for your many curses towards Him.
If you are still Catholic or even Christian,
God will not save you.
No matter what religion,
You have bad, black karma, any God or all the gods would
        Piss on you.
You are doomed to brutality in life,
You have nothing but anger in your heart.
You will be miserable and depressed forever.
So why don't you find that next man who will lie
To you for some pussy or some cash
Someone who will put up with you
In order to take from you.
I feel better and better until
You re-enter my life and fuck it up.
Stay away - smelly, kill yourself, move back to Texas,
Get the fuck out.
You are a waste of life and if your God does exist
He would have struck you down
        Already.
You have a nasty body and
You leave a destructive path wherever you go.
Adam may have treated you poorly and been wrong
But you have a way to push people to want to hurt you;
More than any other person I have met.

I have met a lot of aggravating people
But you are by far the best at getting
People mad at you.
I would never try to hurt you because the longer you live
The more pain you inflict
        Upon yourself;
Your soul already being in Hell and all.
The longer you live the more pain you
Will bring to others and in that you will hurt.
And they will hurt you due to your
Intolerable personality.
Go fuck another rehab junkie,
Go snort some fucking cocaine, fucking loser.
Get sodomized and shit another guy's cum,
Or let another's drip out of your pussy.
I am not mad that you used a month ago.
I am mad that you did not tell me before we had sex;
Now I have to get checked for STDs,
You dumb whore.
You are so fucking stupid and you have
No talent at anything in life,
Except for fucking up other people's lives.
You distort everything to fit how you think
Something happened.
You are the Queen of manipulating
Events in your life to justify your actions.
You distort your own life to help you
Through your whorish actions.
You thwat, you ruthless whore.
You fucking waste of body,
God should have deleted you to do humanity a favor.
You are the most powerful example
Of why God cannot exist.
Why would God create something that is only ugly?
Why did you tell me all the things that you told me?
You fucked up.
You are the ugliest thing I have ever seen,
You look like trailer trash.
Your body changed,
You look like one of those people from a trailer park
Who are skinny and built but it just does
Not work because
Something is lost in the skin and proportions,
Your body looks old.

Your good looks left with your last chance,
Now you look like a gross high school drop-
Out cunt.
Your pussy smells so bad,
And you have grown into an adult awkwardly.
You are like those child actors who grow up
To become an abomination to the ideal
        Of beauty.
Go suck another drug addict's bloated dick and swallow!
How long did you know your last lover…
A fucking week! You fucking tampon.
You are so dirty, no one will ever love you.
No one will ever love you,
No one will ever love you.
If you peeled yourself to muscle casting away
The dirt of your skin
You would still reek of broken promises
And betrayal and you would still be
Dirty.
One day you will die miserable,
Alone or with someone who only feigns love towards you.
You ruined my first day back at work
By possibly giving me an STD
And you neglected to tell me until too late,
That you used someone else's needle.
I will not go to your funeral,
Better yet I will shit on your tombstone.
I hope you fall the same way you pushed
All those people down.
You never listen to anyone,
You are closed-minded and ignorant.
Gangster bitch Barbie, spoiled brat.
Empusae
Whore, cunt, ugly, manipulative person,
You have no control, no self respect,
Your pussy smells,
Your body has become dilapidated and ugly
You are a betrayer and a liar,
You fucking self-righteous spoiled bitch
Burn, you terrible whore,
To gain trust like that and betray it, you are a fucking
User who kills the souls of those around you,
You have no integrity.

Please if you know this girl,
Stay away she is bad
And she will always find a way to hurt
You, even if you think she cannot hurt
She will find a way!
She should just stick to opening
Her legs and exposing her asshole to all those
Who are chronically criminal,
The fucking social deviants.
Emily go stick a fat dick up your ass
And when you shit out the cum,
Think about how sub-human you truly are,
And think about me.
You belong alone sitting on a dildo
Pretending it's me while I walk around.
I have met, swear to God, a prettier, wealthier,
And more intelligent girl
Who would not betray me and would want
To have a relation with me.
Why did I believe you, I love you.[62]

PART III

I have never betrayed anyone that I have loved.
I have never betrayed someone that has loved me.
I am the embodiment of modern society's goal.
I am becoming so fucking vague.
I am not exaggeratory, I do not lie.
This is real and without any use for self-gain.
          Unlike the media
Which has taken the liberty to assemble the packaged
          Real person.
I drink blood.
Eat frogs.
Kill gnats and flies with bug spray.
I am a vegetarian and my pets are getting old anyways.
I hate everyone and boils would help keep them away.
I like to play in the snow and my house is sturdy.

---

[62] 11/16/02: I am sorry if you find this section offensive but I wanted to leave in all aspects of my mania to give the reader a full example of someone manic. In this verse I basically attack women, not just Emily. I listed anything that I thought might offend any woman, in an effort to get out all my rage towards Emily and everything she stood for and against. I was enraged that I trusted someone new and she betrayed me just like my past abusers. I was frightened by the prospect that society was truly filled with evil people.

I am not afraid of a fucking locust; I eat fast food.
I already feel the darkness,
So it would only be mood lighting.
I am not afraid to die.
Abraham is not my father, Isaac,
Or that betrayer of Esau: Jacob.
     I am not a son of Israel.
There is no trinity.
The father created nothing.
The son had no wisdom
That did not result in more death than life.
The holy ghost never existed.
There will be no end lest we nuke ourselves.
God's divine plan,
Takes away the idea of people's individual free will.
Perfection is lost
By rationality and reality, technology, biology.
I am a fucking lion and a fox.
I stopped dreaming because I need not.
There are no fucking spheres or circles or purgatory,
Only nothing.
     I'm just fucking around.
God did not give me the three gifts,
My soul will die, I am too ugly to look like him,
     Society stole my free will.
Fuck you, I hate everyone.
The true nature of human kind pierces society
In these words
Like the many stars in the sky piercing
The blackness of the universe.
So kill me and let irony be in the smile of my dead face.
I know that they will come relieve me so that I can live.

I am grandiose and going mad.
I have trouble losing my thoughts of religion.
My friend let me borrow his modified M3.
I drive down the highway at 130
Listening to 'Head Like a Hole' by NIN
     On my DVD player.
The lights are flashing in my car like a strobe light
     Blinding people in short bursts of light.
People honk their horns and flash their lights.
     All I can think about is everything.
Some of the work has been done to my car
The super charger will be on next week.

The dam broke, the flood began.
I am flooded with emotions
That are making me as happy as miserable.
I think that I am writing like a God.
        I think that I am writing like shit.
Sometimes I think that I am invincible,
Ten minutes later I want to overdose.
I fucking love it right now because
I am in the right place
But that will change as it always does.
Religion, finding a new girlfriend, getting drunk.
My thoughts are furious and eating my soul
        Like a million ants on a dead wolf.
I want to get some models and make them pose.
I want to take pictures of myself
To represent my feelings.
I sit low in the car, my baseball cap tight
        My body burns,
I hit the brakes so hard, the car shakes.
I imagine the gaps in the traffic
While somebody in some supped up Honda
        Tries to keep up.
That corny wing and loud exhaust do not do shit
He could already be turbo charged and lagging.
I will sip my bottle of water, hit the clutch,
Foot off the gas
Pull the shifter into third at 110 and hit the gas again.
Then I come home at 8 in the evening,
Sweat pouring off my face
        As though I stood in a storm.
I began talking but so fast I stop,
Re-think, and talk again
My parents think that I am just being myself, crazy.
I make a funny joke because I am not making any sense.
I cannot listen to anything that anyone has to say
So they make fun of me calling me inconsiderate.
I am the center and with each breath inward
God shares it with me.
I had to leave and come here to float.
I do not know whether I am going to
Ride my car into a wall at 140
Or save someone through
Redirection towards spiritual enlightenment.
All I can do is write from the heart
And be confident that I will bring insight.

Everyday I want to kill myself.
But I do not because I am a pussy.
Or maybe it is because I want to do
Something before I go.
Or maybe I am indecisive.

This night's melody lulls my suburban neighborhood
The sky holds sight for a billion miles
Mystery and beauty abounding
From this place to the next,
Where the wind does not pass.

The many colors purple,
Are like to me the red.
Yet in electric light, spraying white onto it all.
A person receives word from his wife,
'She thinks she's pregnant'
Colors allure,
Catches with it my straying eye,
Will the lazy edit still let me be
Sitting on a brick castle.
All I see is purple.
Like so many first date kisses.
Happiness passes onto me.
In an awkward confusion, I lie to myself.
Let there be black and white.
Let the moon shine white.
Let opposites once again rule the changed field.
I wish to be both and one the same.[63]

I want to live.
Like so many of us still walking, still doing our chores.
My life just changed from then to now.
I am tired from hard work.
Trying to save a corrupted child's mind.
Trying to do something for someone to break a cycle.
Will it be seen more in the bunches I help at school,
Or will I be made a monster for what I wrote about Emily,
I do not know
Who may hate me now and who may love me now.
I do not know if I am a good person
      Or bad.

---

[63] 11/16/02: I was relieved while writing this verse because I was thinking about the extraordinary joys of the grandeur life and death.

In the schism of time
We all grow better until we die.
Some of us just do not grow fast enough.
All of us do not grow fast enough,
To deal with the mental and physical damage
That time inflicts.
We do not grow fast enough to simply be happy.

WEEK 4 JUNE 2002

PART I

Athena's words ring true,
      "You should find a new girlfriend.
      Why are you waiting?"
My sweet innocent Chloe whose words sing
      Tears into a sleepless blood shot eye.
She is right.
With more to say than any therapist.
My Nubian princess who will truly make it.
I told her that "It's not so easy to get a girlfriend."
She, "Why, every boy needs a girlfriend,
      I see pretty girls all the time."
I should heed her advice,
While she speaks standing taller than me
Because she is on the jungle gym
And I am standing in the dirt,
      She should charge me money.
Chloe was abandoned then adopted then abandoned again.
Now she has love in her new family and love from me
And the rest of the staff
And her friends.
That is all the love a young girl's heart needs.
Chloe still defends me.
The other day she came to my defense
As another member of staff
      Made a joke of me.
The other staff was just messing around
But Chloe saw different.
She cursed as part of her verbal assault
Which usually means a five minute time out.
The other member of staff
Like me understands that sometimes
You should be allowed to loose control
In defense of a loved one.
Later on Chloe gets bored in the class,
"I need to talk to you in the hallway Chloe."
I take her for a walk and tell her why and how
She is going to be a princess
And she tells me exactly what type of princess
She will be.
She tells me she loves me.

125

I respond,
"I love you too,
Now get back to class and do a good job!"[64]

I have so much love in my life yet I choose to obsess.
An adult needs more than friends and parents to love.
I need Emily because I need Steve because Steve
        Taught me I needed him.
Steve taught me to need hurt
Because he made us all familiar.

I see kids who have gone through situations
Similar to mine
I teach them that there is more to life than being angry
And feeling that deep powerful pain.
Sometimes I feel not worthy
Because I am unable to dissipate the hurt
In me.

Sometimes a child will ask to be raped
Because that is all they know.
Sometimes a child will try to rape you.
Always I respond to their inappropriate
Request and I say "I understand"
In response to whatever they say.
Then you tell them "I love you too much to rape you"
or "I love myself too much to let you rape me."
I speak to the best of my ability
To change them for better
Then I let the doctor talk to them
Because there is only so much that I know.

I wish that I could adopt Chloe.
I can't.
She is already happy anyways.
Chloe teaches me so much
Because she thinks differently than me
And she does not repress her feelings
She just says it.

---

[64] 11/16/02: Despite my serious symptoms of mania such as psychosis, I was still able to maintain a normal persona at my place of employment. Once again, it is common for people with bipolar to function relatively normal while experiencing serious symptoms. Additionally, I have never met someone who knows that he or she is possibly dangerous until after the manic episode.

I wish I could adopt each one of the kids who has asked.
But instead I have to say,
"I wish I could adopt you but I cannot."
And they say, "Why?"
"Because you deserve a better dad than me.
They will find a better fit.
Do not worry."

You see I am not so crazy.
Give me the topic of children
And I can write fluidly and calmly.
The pages do not ripple from the force of my waves.
I am not all gone.

Chloe and I sit on the bench.
She makes fun of me, "What kinda jeans are those?"
"What do you mean?"
"You need a belt," she giggles.
"What are you talking about, that's the style." Me
She stands up and turns around with her arms up,
Palms to the sky like a flower, "I wear baggy stuff
But you can't see my underwear." Her
"I'm probably going to get in trouble for that." Me
"You already got yelled at by Pam." Her
"Well Pam needs to mind her own business." Me
"I've done more work on my comic book." Her

And that is the best.
All the kids that I got to write.
Fuck the prudent teachers.
As long as the child's writing does not look like mine,
I don't mind.
So what if the kid says shit or asshole.
That is how 10-12 year old kids talk.
I'm not going to suppress their creativity.

Chloe and I sit on the rug during free time
At the end of the day
And we do comic books based on Calvin and Hobbes.
I have gotten some of the other kids to write too.
I got one little girl to write a screenplay
But eventually
It got so ithyphallic that I told her
I could no longer help her with the editing.
        I did not discourage the endeavor.

Hopefully I do not get published because if I do I
        Will be lonely without a job.
I am so proud of the amount of children
That I have encouraged to write.
Sometimes children from other classes
Bring me their projects because
I am the only member of staff that will
Allow profanity in writing.
Chloe is a talented artist too,
Many times I look at her comics
And I think that she is already writing
        Better and more creative versions
Of Calvin and Hobbes.
She writes better and draws better than the creators.
One time I watched a child write a comic strip
Entitled at the top:
"Calvin's Adventures in Ice"
I saw on the cover page a picture that looked like
        Calvin was holding something on his belly.
I read the comic to find out what the premise was,
To quote the child,
"Hobbes kicks Calvin in the testicles."
I said, "Well that explains the ice."
Another member of staff found the comic
And disciplined him.
I believe that I get to work with
The smartest kids on earth.
The crazier the smarter,
The more prismatic the individual can see.
Athena truly looks at the world like no one else
And for that each one of her ideas is genius.

Maybe Emily is a child to me that I wanted to help.
Maybe all I know is how to help.
Maybe I only hate myself because
I failed so miserably at protecting Emily.
I could not protect her from drugs, diseases, hurt.
I have more control with the children.
I am not a member of a team trying to help Emily.
I am her ex-boyfriend.
Shit, Chloe could tell me that.[65]

---

[65] 11/16/02: While manic people can be somewhat introspective.

Numbness is the worst of the feelings.
That is why I think that Hurt by Nine Inch Nails
Is the best, most insightful poem ever written.
He says in that song how I feel better
Than I can express myself.
Probably better than I will ever be able
To express myself.
Hurt is a genius song,
A celebration.
I just hope that I do not skew Reznor's meaning
I am only stating what I got from the song.
Fucking, I need to hurt, I would give everything I have
Which is nothing, and I am sure I will make you hurt.
His song is as good as any Shakespeare. Better.

Fucking car, pretty girls. It is all relative
        The money: someone has a lot more.
My dick is still not going to become bigger.[66]

I need something that is beyond my ability to understand
I am just worried that without that something
I will end up
        With less than what I already have.
I wish you could call me now and save me.
This cut in my soul is growing
And consuming my attention.
I need only to help and have a lover.
But like everyone else in this world
I have been confused;
Confused by the media,
By my peers, by teachers, by abusers, and everyone else.
I believe that I need more,
I need to help the children
And I need someone who loves me.
        Someone other than Emily.[67]

---

[66] 11/16/02: I was frustrated with male competition. [67] 11/16/02: I was depressed while writing this verse. I fluctuated very quickly, intensely, abruptly, and without reason from depression to mania as the weeks passed.

PART II

I know that my writing in respect to poetic value
Does not balance the scale.
Here I am again.[68]

The same place as I was a little while ago.
The singular provocation which opens a dam.
A justified expression of hatred
Emanating from the still parted flesh.
You think you grow but you can only hope
That you have changed.
My destiny based upon an explosive action
And a hope to catch the feel of a point in time,
Of a generation that is complicated and misunderstood.
There is something: I can hope.
During the seemingly eternal darkness of this emotion
I reached into the frigid air
And grabbed a small piece of what was once a whole hope.
The ceiling may rain in on me while I try to save a child;
Or I may sin, between legs, drunk while I extend outward.
I do not believe that everything is going to be alright.
I try to relate then educate to prevent.

India's government spawned from democracy,
Was killed by religion.
Pakistan will get nuked.
That Hindu caste system is the demon
That penetrated democracy.
Now after many years the above couple
(Hinduism and democracy)
Has produced a dysfunctional family.
The Arabs too; both put too much emphasis
On religion in government.
Christian and Jewish people have produced
Happier families,
Christianity by far being the best family,
Christ is a good husband to Democracy.
I am happy to be a son, in this great family.

---

[68] 11/16/02: The grandiose feeling I had resulted in a poor analysis of my book (thus far) for which I had such high hopes.

Though I hope one day,
Because of my time-based distortion,
To leave this family and live peacefully
Around my brothers and sisters;
Parents, grandparents, and great-grandparents
And great-great-grandparents.
I trust in the humanity of my family
To do the right thing,
Without the parents of government and religion.
Times have changed, we have changed.

I must have loved her.
Not her but the other one (Kim).
Once sent to the hospital because
She says 'Shane is crazy,' to my mom.
Now sent to the hospital because another says
'I used a dirty needle.'
Why does everyone that I love outside my family
Betray me?
I have never seen a true friend.
I never had someone to talk to for longer
Than the duration of a stay in the mental
Institution.
I have met a lot of people, tried to be a good person,
Almost always succeeded,
But my male friends walk away quickly.
The females stay long, then stab me.[69]

There are certain things that all of us do.
Out of all the things we share in common,
Perhaps the most profound of all is that
Not one of us understands
What we all share.

I do not hate gay people,
I just speak in a dialect that is offensive.
I call weak people fags and say 'that's fucking gay.'
I would not be pissed if someone said
'That is so fucking Jewish,'
When someone was being cheap to another.

---

[69] 11/16/02: The reader should note that I have a mixed type bipolar. This passage was an example of the rueful, fast thoughts of mania combined with the sullen, hopeless feelings of depression. Most bipolar people I know feel these two emotions at separate times; usually with weeks or months separating the two 'polar' opposite emotions.

I would not be offended if someone said
'That is so fucking Italian (or Ginny)'
When someone went tanning and bought a lot of tacky gold.
I guess that is just the way I was brought up
And that is how my peers impacted me.[70]

No one loves me, I wonder if anyone ever did,
I wonder if I was ever loved not out of commodity.
One person acted like they always wanted someone better;
And the other one though through actions, not words,
Acted like they always
      Wanted someone better.
Listening to 'Portishead' until four in the morning
In 98,
With Kim
Or trying not to love so much in 02
With Emily.
I am an idiot for loving.
I hate myself above all; for thinking.
I am an oxymoron.
I am lost.
I am still looking.
After I was hurt, I became guarded.
Then I had to be hurt again, I wonder if I was guarded,
Too guarded to learn that it is better
To just let love take over.
I wonder if from my youth all I know is pain.
I wonder how much I miss it.
I think I liked it.
I liked to be fucked, it was a new experience
And some of it felt good.
Now I am fucked, I hit puberty as he hit my ass.
Why do I have a burden like this to bear?
Why have my thoughts run away?
You watch love leave and are not prepared because
Manifestations of fleeting love manifest
Into incomprehensible defeats.
Trust you are good.
Kim:
If I did it again I would have chosen love,
And that truly pisses me off
      More than anything Emily ever did.

---

[70] 11/16/02: My thought patterns were not only fast but also non-linear. This means that one verse usually does not have anything in common with the previous or following verse. My mind would go from one thought to another quickly and without provocation.

132

Words spill like a bottle of champagne
Being poured on my stripper's breasts.
I am truly the way that is truly sober versus
The drunkenness of anger.
I feel better to attack than to accept my own failure
My failure of holding my love back,
Never showing her my true love
Because I was afraid, shoot myself in the balls;
And this is much more embarrassing
To write than 'fucking whore Emily'
So I will leave the ratio.
Now? I hope not to repeat the cycle
And I am ready to love.
Let you hurt me;
There is no sense working hard at nothing.[71]

I stopped thinking straight.
I am gone, my connections to the past
I am doomed, to get lost over and over.
I cannot think straight, so I punched through the wall.
I took twenty something klonopins,
I was revived in both instances.
I scream to my Dad's face and curse out my sister.
The lights are dimming.
The stage is set and all the players have come around.
I would rather die than be numbed by medication.
My drive to be famous, all I want is to be famous
        So after my last week I will make it so.
Droopy eyed from too much klonopin
The color had lost my face and I hoped that I would die
        But I did not.
I stumbled around thinking how to make
Myself independent
I do not want to depend on a medication
Or on my Dad.
My fist hurts and bleeds,
The lights are still getting lower.
And fuck, if one more adult sets up
A fucking block to keep me
From becoming famous, I will fucking kill myself.

---

[71] 11/16/02: My hyper sexuality was able to cast a brief shadow over my rage. My symptoms were evolving and changing quickly at this stage of my life.

I will find my old lithium prescription
And I will overdose
With the same ease that I have written this sentence.
I need help and all people offer me is a referral.[72]

Here my disillusioned self cries in the twilight,
Of my shitty book.
Let someone take me somewhere else where my voice
Falls onto a deaf nation.
The phone would ring and I would answer.
Now she does not call me anymore.
I am more normal than I appear.
Please call me, Emily, I hate you but I can change,
I love you, but I can change.
I am insecure and broken
But I will be rebuilt.

I wonder in that stark moment of love lost,
Where love went?
Did it hide, twist itself into some unseen part
Of my body?
Did I lose it in the pile of clothes in my bedroom?
Did love fall out of my pocket somewhere
      On a trip to a faraway place?
The oscillation of my body shook it free.
Where was love kept?
In my heart?
In my hands, then on a windy day,
It flew away?
Was it kept hidden somewhere in my house?
Did I forget where I hid it?
Was it in a box, was it stuck under my skin,
Inside my veins?
Was it under my skin inside a pimple that I popped?
Was my love kept up in heaven with God,
For Him, to one day misplace, as He did with compassion?
Did God become jealous of my love and steal it?
God became jealous of the idol,
The icon and condemned it most seriously as in the
Commandments.
Did He pry open my tight grip or look through my house
      And find my love hidden under my mattress?

---

[72] 11/16/02: All my thoughts, particularly my raging emotions, come together for a verse about suicidal ideation. Suicidal ideation (for me and others) is glorifying and taking comfort in the idea of suicide.

Did He find my old shoe box full of valuables
And cast eyes upon my love
        And determine it too good for me?
Did God think I was not worthy and crept
Into my house while I was asleep?
Maybe we never lose love, we just misplace it?
Like car keys.
Then in a month after
You had to get a new pair of keys made,
The old keys show up stuck in between the couch cushions?
Maybe love left me while I was looking at something else?
Then I turned back and it was gone.
Now I am looking for love left!
And after a while I settle for something
That looks similar.
Maybe I only thought it was love,
And in reality it was a little bird
Who grew up and flew far away.
Maybe what I thought was love was only
A lesser fleeting emotion?
Maybe I confused love for loneliness,
And it left like all the other fleeting emotions?
Maybe when I was swimming,
My love got caught in the current dragged to sea
And some kid in Europe has my love?
I will say 'give it back' and he will say
'No, this love is mine now.'
Maybe a friend or my family secretly stole my love away;
Because they were jealous and wanted it for themselves?
Maybe love melted in the spring like ice?
Maybe love is a fluid that dissipated,
I will make it cold again and pull together the liquid?
Maybe my love got up and left because I offended it?
Maybe my love flew away because it saw
A better home than my heart?
Maybe my love is there now,
Happier than I could have made it?
I hope my love is not gone forever?
But if it is then - good.
Because I do not sell out for anyone
And if my house was not good enough
        Then love can leave me be.
Fuck love, let it go, I am better than it anyway.

Love could not keep up with me,
It could not root deep enough into my heart
I ran and it fell.
I did all I could do to keep it intact
But in the end, love fell onto the ground and broke.[73]

I owe everyone an explanation.
All the people who loved me.
All the people who were there,
And I cannot give one.
I am myself,
I will no longer censor myself,
I pursue truth at
The cost of dignity.
I trade gold for women.
I am the angry people.
I am not just anything.
I am everything that I hate,
        Without the effort.
Tears will drop, people will change
Or rather grow,
When the truer me steps into a brighter light.
There is nothing here you have not seen before.
A stupid boy bringing down innocent people.
Angering the angry, looking for
The self-indulgence of death,
        Not by his own hands.
I will love someone before I die.
I know that I will love because I will it.
Something different does not necessarily
Make anything at all.[74]

So I destroyed all the bitch's shit.
Emily:
I threw out the shoes, the clothes;
The dress pants and the socks,
The expensive shirt.
I took a pair of wire cutters to your ring.

---

[73] 11/16/02: This verse proves my ability to articulate a complex yet subtle idea and maintain a steady stream of conscious thought despite the increasing severity of my bipolar symptoms. [74] 11/16/02: I expressed a desire that had appeared before; the desire to commit suicide by finding someone to murder me. My goal was to incite someone into a murderous rage by writing offensive verses about personal subjects like religion and society. My strategy on how to commit suicide changes a lot throughout the poetry.

I cut it into so many pieces,
It looked like scrap metal;
I threw the little pieces out of the window
While I drove down the highway.
Your fashion taste sucks.
I am pissed at a lot of people,
But since you are so obviously wrong
And fucked and have inflicted the most recent pain:
I decided to have you get the brunt of everything.
I really, honestly love you more
Than water loves to be wet.
More than your pussy longed to be wet around me.
Instead of complaining about all the smaller
Grey area issues or issues that are hard to talk about,
I can turn to you - someone who betrayed me,
Someone that I trusted.
Come back, I love you.
I lied, I did not destroy your stuff.
Please come back, I love you like the sun loves to heat.[75]

You know it is interesting.
I have suffered so badly sexually and you would think
That I would be drawn back to that childhood disaster.
I am not and it deserves mentioning because
I do not think people understand
How people with this affliction (PTSD) suffer.
I remember being laid down and crying, thinking,
         Being positive
That Steve was going to kill me,
While also feeling myself orgasm into his mouth
He stood up and spat out my own semen onto my face.
He would always stand with
A weapon to my chest and say
'Shane all I have to do is push and you would be dead.'
I thought he was going to fuck me, kill me,
And kill my family.
That is a haunting memory and the more I think about it
         The more upset I get.
I have not developed a good coping mechanism
For my trauma.
My memories rush back, from a touch or a statement.

---

[75] 11/16/02: I continued to struggle, trying to understand the origin of why I needed unhealthy relationships with all my friends and lovers.

137

I get flustered and I redirect my thoughts,
Maybe, now, to Emily.
If I bitch and complain enough about Emily
The ating lessons
There are many things that I think about
Besides Emily when I am upset
 Right now she is a target.
Steve comes and goes at his own will
Affecting everything.
Emily is Steve, she is mean, she hurts me over and over
She scars me and we fuck hard.
I can talk more about Emily than Steve.
I do not have to say anything more about Steve.
 I cannot handle that pain.
Emily may be okay, she is probably fine.
Emily is a melodramatic joke, she did not destroy me.
I think that maybe I am still in love with her.
Steve is inflicting pain while receiving it.
Steve's life must be a Hell beyond my definition
 Beyond my ability to articulate.
I cannot imagine how much pain someone has to be in
 To hurt someone else how he did.
I do not know my age at the time of the rapes.
I do not know the duration.
I only know that my ass is loose.
People wonder why I have such wicked ways.
I am bipolar and I was brutally raped and tortured.[76]

Athena asked,
"Why are you looking at nothing."
"I am sad." Me
A smile turned into laughter.
"Yeah…" Her
Now I smile too.

A few weeks ago another member of staff told me not to
 Play so aggressively on the jungle gym.
Earlier today a child tried to do something
I did and got hurt
Then he blamed someone for pushing him.[77]

---

[76] 11/16/02: I continued to struggle, trying to understand the origin of why I needed unhealthy relationships with all my friends and lovers. [77] 11/16/02: I was afraid that my mental state was affecting my job performance, although in this incident, I made a mistake that many members of the staff make - this mistake was not due to an altered mind frame.

"Oh, Chloe, what do you think about the end of school?"
I said with a sigh.
"I'm having fun." Her
"You know that I am going to miss you." Me
"Are you going to cry?" Her
"Probably, I won't have anyone
To make fun of anymore." Me[78]

We go swimming all the time now.
I love to throw the kids in the water.
Though I am not sure if staff approves.
I hold them under the arm and under the knee
Then I crouch down and bounce up and throw.
Sometimes I have to hold my breath
For a long time because a child
Will climb up on my shoulders and I will hold their hands
Then I pop out of the water and toss them.
They love that.
We got this kite and I had a little boy running behind me
Feeding up the rope until the kite got real high.
We kept on doing long circles up and down the cool beach.
Leaving a set of big foot prints
With a set of little ones right behind
        Both disappeared in seconds.
I said, "It's frustrating to get the kite up
And then watch it come down, no?"
The little boy said,
"It's most fun getting the kite up, lazy man."

I wake up in the morning and eat pancakes
That my mom makes me.
Then I go to work and wake up kids and
Make them pancakes.
I tell them,
"I understand how hard it is to clean your room
        But you gotta do it."
I admit, "Someone usually makes my bed."
And I usually end up making their bed
And helping them clean.
I get to work with some sweetness in the morning.
I wake up children on an all girls unit – ages 5 to 12.
I have never done a morning hold.

---

[78] 11/16/02: I was sad but for a reason that would make a stable person sad. The children that I worked for and had developed intimate relationships with were graduating and moving on.

One of the little girls is so studious.
So when we get bored I say,
"Give me a homework assignment?"
"Write four sentences on how you feel." Her.
So I write and I ask her all kinds of spelling questions
        And all kinds of grammar questions.
She says, "I'm a better writer than you so
I am going to show you how
To do this." Her eyes are fixed and serious. She's 7.
I enforce her belief that she is
A better writer than I am.
Because without grandiosity our dreams
Would be vapid and shallow.

During my wake-ups I do a lot of work
With another girl who is 10.
She cannot read and she cannot count very well,
She touches a finger to her mouth
As she mouths the numbers.
I wish that I had more of an opportunity
To do academic work with her
But she is not in my classroom,
I only see her during wake-ups.
We play cards and she is always talking
About her boyfriend at school,
She has harmless relationships
And I would rather listen to her
Now so that if later she does kiss him or worse
I can stop it, as early as possible.
Sometimes I wish that I got little girl crushes on me
Rather than big girls because this little girl's
Eyes turn all glossy and she stares when
She talks of her boyfriend.
I wish I could make someone do that.
A child's life is a grown man's dream.
You can only love what you lost.

Now I work with a kid who is manic
        But child mania is different.
He gets super high then super low
In a matter of hours or minutes.

Sometimes the 10 year-old and the 7 year-old are together
But the 7 year-old girl is so sensitive to the 10 year-old.

It is incredible the amount of sympathy
That these children
        Learn to have.
They accept everything and everyone.

At the beach I was with Athena.
He walked by a group of kids in high school.
He was all like, "Hey, what's up, yo!"
They did not respond.
Then later at the beach I kept saying,
"Look at that girl in the bikini!"
Then he would dart his head all around,
I would laugh,
And he would give me a playful shove.
He told me, "I want a blow job from one of those girls."
"Kid do you even know what that means?" Me
"It is when a girl puts your dick in her mouth
Until your stuff comes out." He
I was surprised that he knew that much.
"There is another word for that called oral sex,
That is the appropriate word.
Don't have a girl perform oral sex on you.
Buddy, you should not even kiss a girl." Me
"Why?" He
"Because all kinds of bad stuff happens
If you have sex too early." Me
"Are you going to tell on me?" He
"No," I will not because my peer influence
Is stronger than an authority influence
        If I told I would be an authority.
"I didn't do that kind of stuff until I was much older
And the kids I knew that did have
Sex young, got into trouble.
They got diseases, their parents yelled at them.
Some of them got beaten up by older people,
Some had babies.
You wanna have a baby?" Me
"No." He
"No one wants to wait for sex.
Sex is fun, I'm not going to lie, but you have
To, have to, wait.
Please as your best friend tell me you are going to do
        What is right." Me
"Okay I won't do that stuff." He
"Good, cause I'm worried about you,

141

Tell me again why so that you are not
Just doing something because I told you to." Me
And he spoke and I honestly believed him.[79]

Last night
I went over to my friend's house and we went clubbing.
I drank three beers which is not very much.
We went to some upscale club next to Fenway Park
We got to see the girls with fake tans
And glittery make-up.
The girls' complexions looked like dark skies
Dripping with stars.
The men all wore shirts way too small
And sported stupid facial expressions.
I was really quiet.
My friend introduced me to these two women
He was talking to
He sported a stupid expression and designer clothing.
I walked away from them because I thought,
I knew,
That this would create mystery, allure.
The girls were nice looking, both had thin legs
They were wearing tight clothes and they glittered.
One girl was black, she was really cute
One was white and she was cute too.
All I was thinking about was Emily
And picturing her fucking,
So prevalent was this thought, I could not think about
What these girls would look like naked,
Much less the feel of
        Fucking one of them.
Because that is what a man does,
He thinks of you naked, that comes first
Then if he likes what he sees he approaches
Or continues pursuing you.
I stood about fifteen feet away
From these girls talking to my other friends
Most of them just did not have the balls
To approach these two ladies.
I stood there for a few hours and then I found
My good friend and said I wanted to leave.

---

[79] 11/16/02: Please note that as I wrote previously, I apply Athena to both male and female children due to my understanding of Greek myth while writing this poetry.

I felt normal, grounded,
I felt ready to go home and get some rest.
My friend started talking to me about
This escort service.
He had drank a lot more than me, maybe 7 or 8 drinks,
Though he was not drunk.
He continued talking about this escort service
With 'ethnic girls.'
He talked about how he and a few of our close
Acquaintances had
       Fucked one in his apartment.
I was interested because without any work
(By 'work' I mean no attempt at courting another lady),
I could brag to Emily about fucking another prettier,
Wealthier girl and I could provide details.
At least that is what kept on circling through my head,
I'm lying again, that is not how it happened
What really happened was my friend
Was eluding to getting a prostitute all night.
I thought little about it, if anything at all.
Then he hopped in the car and said
'Do you want to pick up a hooker to share.'
Before he got the sentence out I said 'Yes.'
It was a total impulse reaction,
There was no reason for me agreeing to have sex
       With a prostitute.
Then the thoughts circled
And I went from not caring to obsession.
Obsessing about what I already stated,
My plot of revenge at Emily.
I thought
"I am a bad liar and this woman would provide
The little details for me to throw in Emily's face.'
I was still physically present with my friend
But I was gone.
I remember this as I remember Vegas,
A movie which I directed.
I see only from the outside.
So we proceeded to elicit women on the street
In areas that hookers hang out at.
I kept saying
'Come in' but my friend drove away and told me
'She was nasty'
I cannot remember their faces.

Next, my friend suggested we turn to the yellow pages
We got back to his apartment at 2 in the morning.
We both were wide awake at this point.
He seemed embarrassed to call
So I said that I would do it.
I felt funny on the phone,
'Do you want red hair, blonde, or black?'
'What dimensions do you like?'
I did not know what to answer.
I cupped the phone and asked for help.
After being walked through it, I ordered.
Then I further flooded, I fucked up even more.
Fifteen minutes passed and no one showed
        So I called another place.
No show and no call again after
About forty-five minutes.
My friend had snuck off into bed
At around quarter to 3 AM.
I felt more alert than ever.
I felt like I was on a fucking mission
        I felt like I was in a do or die situation.
I called half of the agencies in the book.
Girls kept calling back on my cell phone and I lost track
        Because they all said the same thing.
Something like 'Do you want a date' or
'Do you want a massage, 80 dollars.'
I was reeling now,
And I was sure that five groups of people would show up.
I had ordered two girls from many places.
(No more than 1 car with 2 actually came)
I went down to the ATM at the end of the block
For some more money.
I had several hundred dollars,
It was approaching 4 and my friend
        Was fast asleep.
I was pacing back and forth grinning like an ass
All I could think about was how I could humiliate Emily.
I had all these great ideas about how I would say
I was in the VIP room
Of some high class club
When I approached the most beautiful girl.
I would talk about how I charmed her with my rapier wit,
How I made her laugh
And how she thought I was really smart.

All girls, Emily included would ask,
'Was she as pretty as me'
I would say,
'Well… I cannot really answer that…
You two look so different,
Yeah, you are prettier in your own way.'
This would piss Emily off more than anything
Because she would not think I was
Trying for revenge, Emily would think I found someone prettier
I would play on her insecurities
And she would think I was pitying her.
That would be great.
I kept thinking through it,
Pacing back and forth smiling, I must have looked
        Like a fucking idiot.
4:30 came, I kept calling, 5 came, I kept calling.
The sun began coming up and each group of girls
Had the same story
'I'm five minutes away.'
Then at around 6:30 there was a knock on the door.
I was sweating with anticipation,
I was glossed and wide-eyed
My friend was angry when I woke him up.
My friend said he was going to stay in bed.
I felt like my heart was coming out of my chest.
I ran down the stairs and answered the door.
There were two girls, they were not unattractive but
Not nearly as good looking as Kim was or Emily.
One was wearing an ADIDAS jump suit.
The other who looked older was wearing
A fur coat and jeans.
The one in the jump suit was really
Quiet and seemed very young.
        She did not speak at first.
The older one who was maybe thirty
Or a little younger walked
Behind me up to the third floor
Where my buddy's apartment was.
We opened the door and to my surprise my friend was up
Rubbing his eyes and saying,
'How long are you going to stay, how much.'
Some other things were said.
We both paid 150 per girl for a half hour.
My friend and I left the living room for a second
To decide who to choose.

I was impulsive, I did not care, he chose.
I got the young one, we stayed in the living room,
He left with the older one into his bedroom.
She asked what I wanted to do and she listed the prices.
I looked at her and guessed her age at 20 or younger.
Her eyes where shallow,
I have not met a lot of hookers
But I have met a lot of dancers
And a pro has deeper eyes than a galaxy, like Jess.
Jess would have made these girls
Look like beat up rag dolls.
You could look into Jess's eyes,
Know she was going to take you for all you were worth
And at the same time know
There was nothing you could do to stop it.
Jess was perfect, huge fake boobs, so thin and tan,
Her complexion was perfect
        Consistent over her entire body.
She would attract serious attention.
Jess is a model now on TV
And she played a role in a popular movie.
The girl across the room from me
Was an inexperienced moron.
She was stupid looking and I began to feel a hit
        My emotions flared.
It was as if I went from watching a movie
To being inside it.
I started to shake and she asked
If I was okay and I said yes.
I could not have sex with her,
I did not have sex with Jess, no more than a few kisses.
I never want to have sex with a fucking prostitute,
'What am I thinking?'
I asked her if we could just talk.
        We did but I forget what about.
My time went up, my friend came out
Grinning like an ass.
I said good-bye and she walked out.
I woke up thinking what the hell did I just do,
I need to be smarter than that.

My friend called and told me one of the hookers
Had stolen his brand new Mercedes
His keys were missing
And we had left the room for a couple of seconds.
It made sense.[81]

My writing is so masturbatory and self-indulgent
But it feels good to fuck and to be complimented
And in the absence of both I look inward.
Every time I lose,
Something else gets taken away
Because I open my ears and eyes.
I feel bad for many of the things I do
I hope that my mistakes do not end up taking me.
At least let me live long enough
To walk with my parents and sisters.
I wish that I could have shown them hugs.
I wish so hard that I could have cuddled
Or just been more open.
When I was young I felt like a failure.
I am a monster too dark for the words
To be printed deep enough to express the depth
Of my rage;
            I cannot handle the guilt.

---

[80] 11/17/02: I would like the reader to note that this was the one and only time I have ever called a prostitute.

LAST WEEK OF JUNE 2002

PART I

I am fucked up,
I do not know right from wrong.
I do not have morals,
Just the evaluation of each situation as it comes,
Treat you right, treat you wrong.
I am not holding anything back anymore,
Even though I inherently will.
I am you, I am all of you.
You in high school, you in college,
You recent graduates, you in your thirties and forties.
Only a different life separates our similar core
And despite some fear, it is okay.
With the exception of my strange trauma, I am you.
You were probably traumatized too
But in a different way, you and I have so much
      In common.
You are fun, fuck that whore, fuck that man!
I am you.[81]

I feel it, the surge has descended upon me.
Like the prickly feeling on the back of your neck,
      I feel the prickles all the time.
I know it, I know that I have something.
I am doing such a great fucking job.
I see my pay stub and it says 63 hours worked in a week
      And I am doing so much writing and reading.
Depressed or not.
I was informed of an award that
I would receive from my job.
I can make a kid go from the verge of destruction
To settling and going back
      And doing school work.
I can relate without actually
Relating my past or present.
And through me I watch them grow.
I see my colleagues and I do miracles every day.

---

[81] 11/17/02: I continue justifying my bizarre behaviors by drawing a connection between the ways that all the people felt when in emotional pain; I continue to justify myself because I (psychotically) believed that most people felt and acted like me but did not tell others. Again, I often disagree with verses I wrote while manic.

148

I am, despite my constant belittling,
In love with myself.
I love who I am,
I love who I know that I am going to become.
Fuck the impulses, I can handle the rising bills
I have fucked up before and pulled myself back up.
I do not think that there is anything that can stop me.
I am manic,
I would not sell these emotions for fame or fortune.
If I die in this emotion then so be it.
The change happened this weekend.
I woke up on Sunday and found old
Writing to reflect the way I feel now
I thought about adding it but then
I thought it would obstruct the chronology of
This adventure in my life.
I am happy and I think that I am capable of more.
I meet these internists at work
Who go to these great schools
          Like Tufts and Harvard.
I think that I want to go to Harvard.
I think that even at Harvard
I would be smarter than the average freshman.
I know that I am not as smart as
A Harvard Graduate student, yet.
I am sorry about being so fucking high on myself.
It is the disease's fault.
Fucking terrible affliction this disease can be at times.
I am being sarcastic.
Sarcasm is something that I think
May not be picked up on enough in this book.
This is definitely me at a manic time.

I am not a bad person, I am a normal person.
I care deeply about those around me.
I care deeply for all those who are suffering.
I contribute all that I can to help people who suffer.
I think that due to the current state of society,
People with mental illnesses tend to get
Taken advantage of.
I went too far and I was too unclean.
Which is to say I went where you wanted to go
Or where you went but you said
'I never thought that, I never did that,' Phony fuck.

I went to that place that scared you,
You tried to think about it and stopped because
'Normal people do not think that.'
It is scary to be here,
Even though one can watch and take my words in stride.
I wake up every weekday at a quarter to 6
And go to work by 7:30 AM.
Like you.
I get home every day at 6 PM
Like you.
I have a job that requires skill
Like you.
I work with people who are between ages 10-12.
In the morning I work with a larger age group, 5 to 12.
I help them express themselves through
Appropriate means,
Better to shout than to hurt yourself or someone else.
I use behavioral management techniques
To help children be able to
Eventually function in their communities.
I help children that have been abused
A million times worse than me.
Children who are terribly sexually abused
And physically abused
Beyond our ability to imagine
But also beyond my ability to rightly say.
I must above anything else help those destitute few.
Truly, in all eyes,
Which is to say the dozens who know me,
I am a saint,
Canonized by
A suffering child finding comfort in my care.
I am a good person who
Sometimes thinks but rarely does bad things,
Like you.
You have all suffered and
You are all a little manic, depressive
      You are me.

I show the children in my care that they can be happy,
They can make friends
They can be a part of a family,
A group of friends, the community.
Teaching that one day each one of them
Can live a happy, healthy life.

My personal politics need not interfere
With the program's rules and regulations.
I help the children within the parameters of the program.
I do not share my personal opinions
With the children in my care
I use the techniques taught to me by professionals
To help the children
Become more functional, happier members of society.
I am taught how to manage children by a team of people
Who are highly educated and
Have a vast amount of experience in helping children
With behavioral and psychological difficulties.
Sometimes I use my own strategies
And I guess sometimes I break the rules
But I think that everyone does break the rules sometimes
To do what is best for the child in the moment.
My mentors also teach me about how to
Utilize adoption agencies and how to comfort
Children who are in a position to be adopted.
I have learned how to help children
Who suffer from anxiety and other
Problems related to the adoption process.
Being up for adoption is an extremely strenuous
Position for any child.
My objective is to help the children reach
A functional mental capacity
In relation to modern society.
I am.
I sting because I am not a mentally disturbed misfit.
I am a normal looking high society,
Successful twenty-something.
I hope I am like Pink Floyd or
Another great artist who we relate too;
I am the normal person capable of an expression
That evokes a deeper emotion,
Maybe I have a little talent
Or maybe a lot of guts
Or a lot of talent and a lot of guts.
Anyways my hope is to make the readers see
The truth inside themselves and the world.
The ugly place, translated into something prettier to
See how it is even uglier.

The gears are all connected and
Turn the handles correctly and so perfection becomes
The ugliness of monotony and
The lack of expressed personal differences.
To understand the truth of yourself is to gain
A key into directing yourself towards
Greatness; the only foe being the fear
Or ignorance of full personal articulation.
Today people are still afraid to have certain thoughts.
Say certain things.
I did not 'just say it,'
I said it in a way that conveys the frustration of a
Quiet generation, prospective to their feelings.
A connection of many things,
I will lose my job.
I will be condemned by my peers, perhaps
Also by many members of my family,
I don't care.
Better to lead a revolution of free thought,
Lead a person, at least, into an era of faster evolution.
Through time earn back my respect from those
I love and those I do not know.
The freer the more to say, the more to listen to,
The more for you to study.
I am a hypocrite.
I do not have morals,
I invent a proper action
Based on all the pertinent information.
Almost all of you lie to say you have not
Been through ninety percent of this;
Came to the same thoughts, the same conclusions
And were afraid of being condemned for intensity,
Or worse ingenuity.
That is why I want pictures, I want you to see me.
I do not walk funny or talk funny.
My co-workers do not say to me
"Hey Shane, are you manic," because
        I am shaking or sweating all the time.
I have self-control like all of us afflicted.
I do not have shakes or tremors
Or a ring through my nose.
So many people who are not sick still think outside.
The small amount of people who do speak,
Are squashed;

Like flies being swatted by a bible by a person
Who hates gay people because of its pages.
That book becoming again sacred.
They are the ones that will look stupid later.
I am furious, but only in words.
I will contaminate.
I will always be in total control.
I will never hurt an innocent.
I will always help the hurt.
I will never write demeaning statements
About good people.
I will always offer you a hand.
If you hurt me I will strike back
With all my vengeance.
Total love to all that I do not know,
And to those that show me justice.
All hate, and bad wishes to those who
I know and personally dislike.
First of all, fuck the rapist!
The one who penetrated my family to penetrate me.
Second, fuck the attempted rapist cop.
Another trusted figure
With pictures of his kids on the wall, die!
I saw you on the cover of the Herald, fuck you,
How many were there?
Last year at this time while I was in treatment
A chief of police of a town
            Near my town tried to rape me.
He was married and had children
He was arrested and there was a picture of him
On the front page of a popular Boston paper
Being arrested on one account of molestation
            And two accounts of assault.
After he assaulted me last year,
I was so bad to myself, I am lucky to be alive.
It will probably make for a better book
But at another time.
After that overview, I will continue down the list.
Third, fuck you school.
Fuck you teachers who taught me
That I was not good enough.
Fourth, fuck you American Express.
Corrupt company gave a kid with nothing
A 120,000 dollar credit line.

Fifth, fuck those assholes
Who beat me and robbed me at the gas station.
       I am going to find you.
Sixth, fuck all you smaller fucks
That in some way screwed me over.
Fuck you Kim, Emily, fuck you Jess, fuck you, etc.
My blood gone!
Fuck all the doctors who thought
I would need medicine to stay sane.
Fuck the doctors who thought
I could not get up in the morning.
I beat all of you.
I overcame adversity without great help.
Now I do good work for people who really need help.
I follow my training,
I know not to speak of this to my students.
I only teach what helpful people have taught me.
I use strategies I have picked
Up through personal experience,
And I use strategies I was taught by my supervisors.
I have not made anything up,
Or tried to teach anyone of the child
Victims about my provocative opinions.
At my work I excel because of
My wealth of knowledge taught to me by professionals
Combined with my natural and learned abilities
To implement these strategies.
I learn the child, and I use the best strategy.
If I do not know the child well
Or at all and there is a crisis situation,
I am always calm and soft spoken,
I need not do very many holds.
With the unknown child
I try as many strategies as it takes until one works.
I do not believe in yelling,
I do not believe in name calling.
I am opposed to any type of violence on anyone.
Except self-inflicted:
May you be your own judge
And to yourself the only one capable to judge.
I do not think young children should be allowed
The right to kill themselves.
I think people should not have to be hospitalized
For half their lives as an adult,
Before being allowed to take their life with dignity.

I would like to try to get many to be aware,
And also help a few while keeping my opinions to myself.
I am sane but I think about many disturbing things.
There is a time and place, like a journal late at night.
Do not keep yourself inside yourself
And do not think that because you
Think a violent thought, a disturbing thought,
Or have a deep hate that you will
Act on that thought.
This does not exempt you from 're-evaluating'
Which is a most important skill:
Know yourself by writing and/or
Thinking deeply about yourself.
Let your mind travel to the places you do not want to go
And also to places you are afraid
To go, come back from that journey with
The self-knowledge to help you develop
Strategies to be a less inverted hence
A more effective and happier person.
Do not censor your thoughts;
The more you know about yourself the greater the chance
That you can find a happier way to live
And find ways to avoid activities that
Evoke negative feelings, you will relieve a lot of
The heavy weights that burden
You with negative feelings.
Be vocal, tell others, if they tell you
Not to do something, analyze it before condemning
        That action or idea.
Be happy and have fun, be free
And your absence of society's weight will make you
Relieved of that pressure and of that subsequent pain
That so many live in.
Not everyone can be something great,
Be happy to be something
And be happy that you're something that is
Free and as a result unique;
Because in this sense you will be great.
I will not hide my humanity in order to convey
A positive message and retain a positive
Social image,
We all think down a dark path more often than admitted.
My humanity proves the fusion of my reality
With their society.

The dirt, the filth contributes to the understanding
Of the imperfect connection,
        The imperfect perfection.
Dad is only as bad as the action or the threat,
I do bad things but I do not do things that are very bad.
Hopefully by now you know what is bad
And what is considered very bad.
I am explaining myself too much and am beginning
To sound insecure about my position.
This book is designed for mature people
Who are mentally stable.
Fuck it, if you are under 14,
I still think you could benefit from this reading,
If you are 13 or under do not read this.
I am sure you have watched *The Point* on HBO.

PART II

I threw my wooden staff onto the ground;
It became a snake.
I put my hand into my chest and my chest became white.
When I picked up the snake - it turned back into a staff
And when I stuck my hand back into my chest –
My chest became flesh colored
I was not greeted with skepticism
But to my surprise they found magicians capable
        Of the same feats.
There is a hierarchy of emotional impact
Through artistic means.
First and worst is books.
I do not like reading,
Reading fails to take me to another place.
Then television and movies.
TV and movies make me cry
And laugh along with the story line.
Then music, music can make me feel anything
With sound and words.
I listen to music that makes me cry and laugh,
I listen to music that makes me think about things.
Music and TV can be very powerful.
Books do not make me feel so much,
They do not evoke the necessary vulnerability
That music and the medias create.

I want to make you think, just think;
Think about something different and question.
I wish I could make you cry,
I wish I could make you laugh.
I hope that I can make you laugh.
A book has made me think about passionate things,
But lacks something.
How do I make an impression on you?
I have yet to read something to impress emotions on me
To the degree which I
      Wish to inflict emotional reaction onto you.
First I need the premise.
Then I need to express that premise
In a way that makes you feel.
I do not think that I have done that.
I wish I had done so much more.
So here I go with a continuation of dribble,
I can be happy to have the good ideas
But be disappointed at my own uninteresting presentation.
I am starting.

PART III

Chloe is gone.
She graduated earlier today.
I don't want to talk about it.
I tried to teach her as much as I could before she left.
She taught me more.
I got her a big gift because I wanted to show
My appreciation.
I already miss her.[82]

There are many other people I need to care for
      So now I have to transition.

Now we get to go swimming twice a week.
Athena comes, gives me good advice.
She saw me cry on graduation day.
Most of them at least saw me glazed.
Not many of the children cried.
I got this chair that the kids made me.

---

[82] 11/17/02: Whether manic, depressed, paranoid, or normal, I cared deeply for the children in my care and it broke my heart when a child would leave or would feel hurt.

Each child in my classroom drew a picture and
        Signed their name.
One kid wrote burn on it
        And I have a tattoo that says burn
But then I thought back.
One day he asked me to put on his suntan lotion.
So I put it on, I put suntan lotion on a lot of the kids.
The next day he came in
And lifted up his shirt,
"My dad says you put the lotion on wrong."
I looked at the red stripes on his back
And said, "You have to keep your shirt on in class."
I usually don't fuck up the suntan lotion
And I think my rude attitude
Earned me my vengeful drawing.
His emotional development prevents him
From having fluid conversation.
I should have made more of an effort to talk to him.
I would have understood the joke.

The summer should be fun.
I get more responsibilities plus
I get to work with a bunch of young internists.
Maybe I will find another woman to be my girl.
A good woman who is more like me
Who can take care of me as much as I take care of her.

Back to graduation.
I cried and not only did every child not laugh at me
        But every child, every last child I knew
Tried their best to console me.
It must have felt funny to feel my big body shiver
In their tiny embrace.
Usually I feel the quiver when I hug them hard
        During a hard time.
They returned a favor.
They taught me.
They loved me. They consoled me.
I was not so good to them. Though I tried.
I played chess in the back room
        After a child rescued me.
In the classroom I was always vigilant and quick to
        Separate a person in pain from a group.
Save them the embarrassment.
Talk through the issue.

When I played chess with this very bright young man
        He kept on asking, "What's wrong Shane."
He returned the favor.
The sting grew as I had to say good-bye to many people
        Who I loved very much.
I had to say good-bye to people
Who I felt needed more help.
Most of them, however,
Are getting what they need in a new environment.
I cannot put into words the feelings I had
        Seeing those children grow.
They came so far, so fast.
Further than me – faster.
I have cried all day today.
I am crying now
There is no joy greater than seeing a tortured soul break
Free of the chains of their abuser.
I was a peasant among soldiers today.
Truly this day penetrates the solid crust of hate
That burns away my sanity.
Relief through the feeling that I can connect
A thought to an action.
I understand why I am sad and angry today.[83]

I saw less than nothing grow into something,
        Break out of its pot and walk.
My sinister urges beat on
Like the bleeding at a slaughterhouse.

I ate the cake but when I was alone
        I cried into my Sprite.
Like a fallen star.
I laughed today as much as I cried.
It isn't fair.
I cannot reap my harvest.

I am selfish.
There are so many people who contributed to generating
        Bright white emanations from obsidian.
Dust to Diamond.

---

[83] 11/17/02: There are many good programs like the one I worked for and I was not grandiose to think that I had a major effect on certain children. Children suffering from psychological disorders, whether abused or not, would often grow in leaps and bounds once in treatment.

I got to meet the parents of all the children who had.
I got my yearbook signed.
Some of the graduates put their addresses down.
I will write them.
I did not get Chloe's information.
I am tempted to just look it up anyways.
It was painful to see her at graduation
  And I know she will go far,
So I kept away.
I spared myself from breaking down onto all fours.

Driving home, salt impeded my vision on the sunny day.
I have to dedicate today to them.
Though I often forget my truer feelings
During my writing here;
  I get caught in a web of anger.
Today will go and perhaps that is
The most painful realization
  I have to make.
I will
Once again
Have to battle with the perverse connection between
  Anger and energy to abuse.
Because I feel upset even though I know
That new kids will come,
  New relationships will be formed.
I wish I could be close to Chloe forever
  Watch her become a princess.

Right now I am content.
I understand why water tears my cheeks.
I look forward to a summer
Filled with people I care about.
I am content to look at the children's growth and know
  I played a role.
I was there for some of these children
From the beginning of their stay
To the end, watching them become whole and happy.
I watched them enjoy the things that they should enjoy.
I was there and I did something.
I hate that I could not have done more
More for them
More for Emily.

PART IV

I am somewhere up in the sky sitting on a fluffy cloud,
The breeze carries me weightlessly.
I am at peace and in control.
I took more than I give myself credit for taking
People say 'I could have it all.'
No!
Look where I am, I like you a lot Emily
You are a good kid,
I won't say anything else bad about you
I was just pissed about that whole STD thing
      Or maybe just that you were gone
I miss you, I want you back.
Kim, I wish I could have done something
But I forget a lot of what happened
And even with new insight
I cannot apply my new resources
And ideas to a situation I am not privy too.
So much time has elapsed
The sun is further from the earth, though it still spins
Do you know what you are saying?
I know what I am saying.

I got my car back on Saturday,
The day before I wrote this.
325 plus 150 plus 40 plus 25
      I easily have 540 horse power.
I took my car out yesterday to make the feelings shoot
      Through my body like what I imagine
It would feel like for a woman to have an orgasm.
I got those waves and I feel like you, we can relate.
I got in my car and listened
While the supercharger whistled quietly.
My friend has a Corvette and a few times we
Went fast down the steep hills
On the Pike out west near Springfield.
My friend floored the car forever
And the speedometer went past 170 mph.
His Corvette has 355 horsepower.
My speedometer goes up to 155 mph,
The car is whistling in the driveway
And I am climaxing with anticipation,
Though I am not hard.

If I hit the gas at around 4000 rpms the car screams.
It screams like a lion roars, like a war cry
        And the body shakes.
It is a ferocious sound.
I already got a taste of the car's violent nature
But not enough to savor.
Sure I hit ninety or a hundred following my father home
        But I had to let up off the gas quickly.
The pull is like a push someone gives you trying
To incite a fist fight.
Getting ready I pop out my DVD screen
With the new Korn CD in it.
I figure, if I floor it on the way to the highway,
The tires will spin, I will lose control,
And I will die.
With the window cracked enough
To feel the hot summer wind
I proceed toward a vacant highway at 3:30
This Sunday morning.
I am impulsive to the point of psychosis, I again
Lose myself,
But I see myself just out of reach, I stretch
To grab hold and come up short.
I am slightly too far away and the music kills my voice.
I am totally numb and even crazy, confident,
I doubt my judgment,
'Can I control the car, with all the shaking I am doing?'
I do not want to be here right now
        But I have no choice
I have to prove something to someone that does not exist.
I have to prove something to someone
That is not even an imagined entity
I am getting on a rollercoaster, time to let go,
I was an idiot for buying the ticket.
The on ramp comes and I go,
Down into second, hitting 60 around a hair pin turn.
Then I punch it, look down and
See the speedometer reads 130 and
        I jump on the brakes.
There are other people on the road.
I establish where I am and decide where
I will test my limit.
But I am unable to follow my self-instructions.
I can feel my shirt getting wet;

My neck and face are moist
        And I am not going to stop sweating.
I blast the AC.
I decide to take it easy until I get a little further
West where there will be nearly no other cars.
I am cruising at 70 in the passing lane.
There is a car following me close,
Slowing down slightly and speeding up
Making themselves look like they are going to hit me.
I switch lanes and let it pass,
I could tell by the xenon lights that
        The car behind me was not a total piece of shit.
It was a late model Porsche Carrera,
My car stock was about as fast
Though admittedly it could not match
The Porsche's top speed.
Modified my car would kill this thing,
A Porsche Turbo would be competition
But this Carrera was nearly 200 horse power behind me.
I was numb and I came to the top of the coaster,
This was the time to raise up my hands
So I floored it as the Porsche flew by
I hit 140 and was close to topping out in fourth
When I sling-shot
By this fucking guy.
I passed him like I used to pass a Celica;
There was no comparison
And now once at this speed I kept going.
I looked down,
It seemed like a second after switching into 5th gear
And the speedometer had become stuck onto 155.
Cars that seemed a mile away were reached
In a few seconds.
I kept my foot down still,
The car began to feel as though it was being crushed
        The pressure inside increased dramatically.
My ears hurt a little.
I had to have past 185 and I was coming to a big hill,
The car still had a lot of power
My ears began to hurt from the pressure
And my body was drenched.
My foot stayed planted to the floor
My front headlights which were pop up lights
Started to turn straight up
From the wind's sheer force.

I could not see a fucking thing
Except that the whole world was moving backwards
     All the cars were coming at me.
I kept the car floored for several more seconds,
Eventually my driver side view mirror
Flew off and hit my car.
The noise was an incredibly loud bang.
I jumped on the brakes.
I must have hit over 200 mph easily.
There is nothing that compares to that rush.
I drove home and parked my car,
My lights were fucked up and would not close.
There was a huge bump on the passenger side door
     And a little scrape.
I was jumping up and down in my driveway with joy.
I had had so much fun and I felt so alive.
I felt invincible, I felt like,
'I should be careful jumping I might just fly away.'
I woke up today and felt a little shitty.
I could have killed some family
On their way home from something.
I did not want to drive fast at all,
Though I was happy afterwards.
I guess the above statement is one of many
That only a bipolar person could relate to.
I am not me when I do things like this
I am not me on medication,
I do not know how to save me.

So if white fucks red, you get pink.
I want to fuck pink so I can get blue.
Then I will mix my blue until it turns brown.
Then I will throw it away
And wait for red to get fucked again.

You're not Jimmy, Lenny.
Jimmy Hendrix was a really cool innovator.
Plus he was talented.
Lenny Kravitz you are a fucking tool.
I may change
But I will not stay stuck as a loser.
I am a true changeling, I change my clothes, my hairstyle
     My facial hairstyle and most importantly
My facial expressions and my general demeanor.

To each person I am a different person
But I am so confident in
Who I am,
As long as I am not suffering at that given moment.
It is my confidence in change that makes me sure
I am no loser;
No poser, even though I may look like one to the world
        Or at least to people in my own world.
Everyone plays a different role to a different person.
I guess.

I honestly have no respect.
Respect is another word for an honorable lie.
People who fight are brave.
Bravery means facing a fear, win or lose.
I care about all the brave people in this world
And I wish that political figures would stop
Showing us respect
And start showing us bravery
By at least attacking our enemies
Trying to defeat the need to fight.
I need to rest now so I can write a proper ending prose.

It was either this or the porno website.
Within the first page of my website
I would start by stating:
My name is Shane and I have videos of me
Fucking small-breasted Asian women.
Then I would hire some fat cheap fuck to play me.
I will probably have three fat guys named Ron play me.
Staying true to the 'broken promise motif'
Of the 'somehow' poorly done porno industry.
So well funded and so lacking of quality,
No artistic pictures and no good acting.
Or if cheaper than three Rons,
I will get some college kid with a lot of pimples
        Who is strapped for cash
Then have a few Mexican girls wear make up to look Asian.
As I have seen it done so often.

I wonder if any reader will be able to disseminate
My disturbed personality
From my attempts at humor or vice versa.

Why did I not believe her when she said she loved me,
I could have fixed it,
I love you.
I yearn to come back after the reckoning,
Back from a flame
Of fire down into a less radiant physical form.
Heaven could not make you more radiant.
I just want to be with you and only you forever.

To Emily:
(and then I'll stop the downward spiral and cap this novel)
The sweet smell of spring lingers in the air
However, my mind's black cloud distorts the horizon line.

My mind jaded provoked by jealousy
Taken yet again by rationalized premonitions.

I am hurt and not tended to rightly
I am abandoned before I needed a savior, you.

My hallowed soul screams, echoes the others:
My heart and my brain leave a residual effect, absence;
Pulling together the whole of my self.
I am lost but my hurt can be fingered, you understand?
I may not be capable of feeling
I may be feeling more than the infinite black holes' depth.

You are the wind that carries the spring warmth
I am a shadow cast by your flowering trees.

I will write you better, when I am more awake, it's 1 AM.
I will work on something great for you.

TRIBUTE TO MY BEST FRIEND

BEGINNING OF JULY

My adorable pug-nosed pup went away today, July 7, 2002. My best friend and sometimes my only friend for the last twelve years. I hope that he has company in heaven. I hope that he is not lonely. On earth he made me never feel lonely and now I feel like we are both alone. If everyone hated me, my puppy still loved me. If I was yelled at, beaten, or raped, my pug gave me love. My puppy listened to everything that I had to say. When my family made me feel like they abandoned me I still had a friend in him. I have never prayed more for anything than to let him become lighter than a ray of sun and shot to the brightest star. I love my dog so much and now he is sleeping and living inside his dreams. He died dignified. He stood up for as long as he could before the sedative hit and he fought before he collapsed and was euphemized. He was always a brave dog, he was tougher than any animal that I have ever met and he died before anyone could have usurped his power within my house's animal kingdom. I can remember all the long walks to the park and chasing you around. My dog got to see me grow from a very young boy into a man. My dog had more charisma than me. My puppy was my shadow both in sight and in mentality. I am so afraid that my heart knots and falls at the thought that he may be without a friend up there beyond my vision. I sweat and tears split my sun-scorched face. I do not understand why his coherence left him and why he had to walk around in senility for the last few years. Though no fool proved by his relentless pursuit through many an ingenious endeavor for food. Indy underneath an eagle flying over his right side. Indy with a slice of food atop his head. I feel dead without you. May you be happy and never lonely and may I one day find you so we can resume a game of tug of war.

SAME DATE AS ABOVE DIFFERENT SUBJECT MATTER

I just want to see you happy. I do not want people to be led by false perception. I want people to be able to use all five senses in a way that is helpful. I want you to be enlightened. I am having a hard time writing a good-bye. I am having trouble with this whole sentence structure thing. I feel like all I did was spit onto the pages before this one. Now I have to switch gears and be lighter on the pedals. I have written a book of poems and prose in a very short period of time. The catalyst for this endeavor was wanting to get published without caring what people thought. This time I will not try to use big words or small words. I find with my poetry and prose that I end up using less vocabulary as most of the articulation is done on the magnification of the simple to find that hard to express idea or emotion. I will release my awesome work later. If you like this then I really have something great in store for later. I do care deeply about what you think but I could not care less about what you think about this book. If this writing sucks to you, okay, I will do something drastically different next time. I already have much more sophisticated writings in progress. There is no adjective to describe me or my writing style. I felt the heavy weight of many difficult situations pulling me down, I had to lighten my load. Most of what I have spit onto this schism of work are ideas and information that I have never shared with anyone. I feel that we all hold too heavy a burden and that society has much to gain from realists. My ideas are mostly not preconceived notions, they are what I thought in a moment but some of the writing is deliberate. I hate so many things that I feel would offend you, and I love so many things that I feel will offend you; furthermore it is my belief that we share these tastes only you are afraid to share yourself. People are afraid to think certain thoughts. I am sometimes afraid to think about certain thoughts. I think that this method of thought was ingrained in most of us from a young age. I hope that I make you happy, maybe I will make you think and come to conclusions about my writings, or maybe you will want to learn more from my exposure. Pick up Dante's Paradise Lost. Hopefully one could, by shifting through this mess of words, find insight into oneself in order to find ways to build more fulfilling relationships with others and oneself, thus becoming significantly happier individuals.

I love my dog, fuck you Emily.

LAST WEEK OF JULY 2002

PART I

I fucked up.
I wanted to be a superstar, I wanted to be famous.
The models were too expensive.
The lighting effects were also too expensive
For something creative
And besides I wanted to express something.
The same day that I cut,
Is the same day I went back to the Pavilion.
The doctors that stitched me shut at the hospital
Deemed me 'safe' enough to not need
      A locked hospital environment.
I told the doctors why I did what I did.
I guess things worked out for the best
I was going to have a contrived image of
Self-inflicted injuries.
I would have looked so phony if things worked out.
Instead my friend stabbed me
      That put a surprised look on my face.
That made the pictures totally genuine.
I thought the pictures would be contrived
But I never anticipated
Holding my body together, scared of death.
The doctors think I need to be heavily medicated.
I fought them
      Like Athena against Ares;
I fought like Ares.
I came in and my chest was sore
I could not reach my arm above my waist.
The big thick stitches that hold my chest together
Broke the lie of a phantom power inside an angry boy.
Eating yogurt so that the antibiotics
Would not give me a stomachache.
I wish I was dead
God kill a suffering soul, to spare his family the grief.
At night lying in the cold room praying
For everything to just go away.[84]

---

[84] 11/18/02: I had recently suffered about 100 cuts; one could have been fatal. Most were inflicted by myself (but not the worst). When I wrote this passage I was recovering at McLean and had recently been discharged after getting several stitches. A more in depth explanation of the incident is provided in the epilogue.

I left the children forever.
I should have let all this life lead me
        Into a deeper puddle of blood.
I am a terrible person
        And I cannot even bring myself
To talk about my position in respect to the children.
The only people that I have loved,
Maybe truly the only people ever that I loved.

Now I can move a little more.
I drive my car home at night to take showers.
I do regret it
        Doctors tell me I am 'flat.'
I see them everyday, several times a day.
Today I talked about my abuse.
I talked about how I did not cut myself.
I had to take a break from writing.
The stitches bristle against my shirt, I can
        Not hug anyone.
I could not hug a child.
I hate everyone.
I tell the doctors that I am doing great.
All I am is anger.
All I remember is pain.
I will die rather than lose my job.

PART II

They put me on Lithium and I am 'flat.'
The doctor said I would die without it.
I told the doctor all I wanted to do was
Succeed in a creative capacity.
Now I am learning skills to cope better with life
        While the Lithium roots into my brain.
I want to kill myself because the medication
Makes me feel blunted
I cannot concentrate to create.
I never want to die unless I lose the only thing I have -
        The dignity that my perception gives me.
Now I look at the world and I only see figures -
        I used to see life.
I used to be able to think fast and talk fast
        For that I was proud.

I could save the hurt child
    Come up with the quick solution.
You get a second to think, make a wrong move
    The kid hurts you
Or worse the child hurts him or herself.
My wit got my laughs, gave me the power to create plans
    Got me hugs from those little arms.
I miss those bend at the waist hugs.
Now I have nothing to lose.
Without medication
    I race cars and I cut myself.
I will accidentally kill myself off the medications.
I am useless to myself
And to those I love on the medication.
Either way I am destined to die young.[87]

I do not want to die,
But I think I could kill myself trying to become famous.
Everyone says I have a crazy look in my eyes
In those pictures and there is
    No doubt that I was and that I am insane.
I was not that drunk, I did not do any street drugs
    I wanted to take a picture of how I felt.
I did not cut myself that deep.
It would have been impossible.
I stood there and I can remember holding
My own guts and saying
'I need to go to the hospital,' while he said
'I need to take a picture.'
I meet with the doctors everyday to tell them how I feel
    And the doctors tell me I need help.
If this book is not a testament towards
Early intervention
For people who have psychological problems
I do not think that such a book exists.
I am crazy, I need help,
Forget about everything else I said
And watch the people around you that you love.

---

[87] 11/18/02: Lithium makes nearly everyone I have talked to feel less emotional. Lithium took away my mania, though in this verse, my depression was intense enough to have possibly resulted in my suicide.

You see the circle – it is more painful than ever:
If someone had watched out for me
I would have watched out for these children
These children would have had a better chance.
I am not stating that I am a savior but there are not
Very many people willing to do the work I do.

PART III

My book, she is shallow.
I thought about adding parts from the past
      To fill in the gaps
My disease made in the future.
I could not disrupt my flow.
It is impossible to write of such a disease in its entirety
     In one episode.
The mind gets lost.
I am full of a million damaged thoughts
     I cannot salvage even a piece
Of what I was.
I could not speak my piece because
All my pieces were not together.
     This is why
     I needed to
Reference my past.
Everything I forget to say then,
     Coupled with what I forgot to say now.
They cohere to the full episode.
Without the past, my future makes no sense.

I met a doctor today.
A good one, he likes me.
I can tell – he knows I am an oddity.
I looked him up on the internet
President of National Institute of Mental Health
Former President of McLean
Profiler of violent criminals.
I fascinate him,
He is different from all the rest of the
Doctors and people
That I have met.
He sees and hears things that no one else can
His senses are infinitely higher than a regular person's.
He sees me lying and he knows it

I am just waiting for him to say it.
For him to say, 'who cut you' and 'who raped you.'
Maybe he will end up helping me.[86]

I was too busy to write for a while.
I was helping and teaching.
I got some really insubordinate kids
        To listen to direction.
I got children to stop being violent
        To themselves
        And to others.
I got a lot of hugs
Tight ones where the kid did not want to ever let go.
I went away.
I stayed for a year and then in the time of a blinking eye
        I abandoned them.
I left them to face a world that I could not face.
I left some of them alone, ruined their trust.
I love them.

---

[86] 11/18/02: I was referring to Shervert Frazier in this verse.

FIRST WEEK OF AUGUST 2002

PART I

I fucking hate myself.
I can feel the depressive side of me taking over.
I do not care how contrived I sound.
The whole fucking time that I was in the hospital
      I had to pretend I was someone else.
And it worked because I was working.
I am off the Lithium,
      I was on it for about a week or so.
I cannot fucking handle it
Like I have said and alluded to so often before
'Better to be dead, than to feel nothing at all.'
My cut,
My cut was horrible and it scared everyone
But I did not mean to cut so deep.
I made a mistake; a few cuts
And one main cut that I acknowledged might need stitches.
But my cut split me in half
      The blood poured like a faucet
From the top and from the bottom.
The middle was a translucent slime.
      I touched it and so stayed inside
While the rest stayed on my hands.
My guts were falling out.
Now the stitches are out
And I have a fucking dent in my chest.
I cut myself between 90 and 110 times,
      I counted.
My friend cut me once, a fourteen inch cut
Starting under my arm pit, between my arm pit
And my belly button
And going up diagonally to the opposite side's
      Shoulder blade. A huge cut.
That was the only one in and of itself
To be capable of being a fatal wound.
My friend said I lost a liter of blood
In less than a minute
      My body was red
Like an American Indian.
My bed sheets got ruined
Because I slept for about 3 hours before going in.

I sat on the table in the hospital
With three security guards
    And my wound exposed
My body was pulling against me so hard.
I am depressed now and I do not know it because
    I have grown tired and
I have a lack of interest in things that I love.
None of that DMV4 symptoms of depression bullshit.
I am depressed because I was hit
    Like a sledge hammer against my brain
My head aches like there is a worm in there
Rotting it out.
I hate everyone, people I liked or even loved a week ago
    I have no patience for.
If someone pisses me off - I go off
    I throw things
I hit walls and sometimes I cry.
I hate myself but I will not kill myself because
    This will pass.
I still think about doing something around
    Helping those little people that helped me
    For the last year.
Lithium will never pass unless it is out of my system.
I was still manic for several weeks after I cut myself
I know because I was still functioning highly
Had the hospital car take me to my publishing lawyer.[87]

I got the courage to start calling contacts
At my school again.
I am going to visit in a few weeks.
They do not know what happened but I am confident
That when I talk to them they will still view me as
    A good human services worker.
Because I think I am.
Hope and anger come and go in this mind frame
    I just hope that I do what is right
When it is most important.

I liked the people I was in the hospital with
    And would often stay up late
Talking to them, helping them with their problems.
Now everyone I liked there is gone.

---

[87] 11/18/02: I continued to show serious symptoms of mania three months after the onset of the episode.

I kicked my fucking printer into
Pieces because that fucking
Thing got jammed up so many times.
I can only say one thing before I crash
I can only say this one thing about my
Manic episodes as well.
God, if I die do not let it be trying to achieve
An artistic vision
Do not let me take my own life in a moment of despair.
God please, if I am to die
Let it be by saving someone else
      For I would rather be crucified.
I would rather feel the spikes enter my arms and endure
      All the other tortures
For a chance to save another
For a chance to make another happy.
Let them beat me, let them rape me,
Let them leave me without dignity
      Or pride
Just let me die in a way
That helps someone else feel happy.
Good-bye[88]

I am not intelligent enough to
Find the words that mean how I feel.
I must quote someone smarter than me
In dedication to all my failure in respect
To my students and Emily:
I am sorry if I fuck up the words,
They are different at different websites, therefore,
I am writing them down
In the way that they hit my ear while sung.[89]

---

[88] 11/18/02: A perhaps notable point is that my poetry had become more obtuse in July and August. I am not sure why this phenomenon occurred; I could blame medications or the onset of depression or even that I was preoccupied with therapy or that my mania was waning but I am not sure of the antecedent to my simplistic verses. [89] 11/18/02: I felt like I let everyone down and that makes me depressed. I wanted to express my depression but I could not find powerful enough words.

HURT – BY TRENT REZNOR
I hurt myself today
To see if I still feel
I focus on the pain
The only thing that's real
The needle tears a hole
That old familiar sting
Try to kill it all away
But I remember everything

What have I become my sweetest friend?
Everyone I know goes away in the end
And you could have it all
My empire of dirt
I will let you down
I will make you hurt

I wear my crown of shit upon my liar's chair
Full of broken thoughts I cannot repair
Beneath the stain of time the feeling disappears
You are someone else
I am still right here

What have I become my sweetest friend?
Everyone I know goes away in the end
You could have it all
My empire of dirt
I will let you down
I will make you hurt

If I could start again
A million miles away
I would keep myself
I would find a way

EPILOGUE

DECEMBER 2002

Perhaps I have disappointed some people with the ending of my free-style journal. I am sorry that I was not able to write more about my recovery from the illness; I am still recovering. I am sorry that it doesn't include a happy ending. I spent three weeks at McLean and I did not gain anything worth mentioning. My recovery is stated in this final section. I descended to a deep, dark place last summer, and I am climbing back out much more slowly than I fell in. But I still hope that one day I can write a happy ending. I hope that one day I do overcome my disorder or at least become less symptomatic. That day may come soon, but that day is not today.

I have a serious condition and I have been away from myself for many months. Although I am not fully recovered, I feel that I am making clear progress in understanding my thoughts and behaviors that have negatively influenced me over the course of my lifetime. I do not have an answer to every question, of course. I will never be able to answer a lot of the questions I have about my thoughts and actions, but I can hope that with time and therapeutic guidance, I will resolve most of my issues.

Unfortunately, I cannot thank the Pavilion at McLean for helping me gain a deeper sense of self-perception. I wish this was not the case because I do not like having yet another institution to be mad at and I do not want to come across as someone who is angry at everything in this world. I am not filled with hatred all the time as my free-style poetry suggests. I am upset, however, about spending close to sixty thousand dollars and three weeks in this program and only getting three pages of typed information, one handwritten document that no one could decipher, and a bunch of papers indicating that I tested negative for illicit drugs in my system. I could not find any guidance or insight within those pages. In all honesty, the Pavilion report infuriates me. I would expect that for the amount of money I paid and the information I shared, I would at least receive a comprehensive report that would provide both a better understanding of my illness and some guidance for dealing with it in the future, and perhaps also some comfort.

I would no longer recommend the Pavilion program to anyone. If you are in a crisis and are very wealthy, I suggest that you participate in therapy at McLean Hospital and see some of their doctors, but the Pavilion is not going to help any more than a good team of a psychiatrist, a psychologist, and a social worker. One might also consider the possibility of attending some groups on the McLean campus.

In addition, the Pavilion is terrible for young adults or anyone who does not have their own source of income. The Pavilion's doctors cater to the needs of the person with the money, not to the person suffering the illness. Parents will recommend a less intensive treatment plan than what the patient needs. I sincerely believe that this will result in many patient suicides. The Pavilion disregards its morals for monetary gain.

In addition, the food is not very good at the Pavilion, and I calculated the average

179

cost per appointment to be over eight hundred dollars. I do not understand that figure. I do not know anyone who pays a doctor 800 dollars for a one-hour appointment. I must, however, credit one McLean doctor who is not part of the Pavilion team with helping me a great deal with my ability to rationally understand myself through deductive reasoning. I would call this doctor my friend before I would call him my treater. He is a great man whom I admire as much as I have ever admired anyone. The name of the doctor that I have been working with is Dr. Frazier. He has been treating my bipolar illness by helping me to better understand the origin of my illness. Through understanding the origin of my illness I can begin to rationally deconstruct my negative thought patterns. Most of the Epilogue has been generated through meetings with Dr. Frazier. With a better understanding of my illness, I am more able to detect early warning signs of a potential disaster. Perhaps I should explain to the reader at this point the specifics of bipolar as to provide some light into some of the issues I have been dealing with and also help people in general understand bipolar illness better.

My bipolar, is not, as might be assumed, the result of trauma in my life. Post-traumatic stress disorder cannot create a bipolar person. People are manic for many reasons, usually the disease is genetic and provoked by certain drugs and medications. The symptoms of my illness do not fall into any specific categories of bipolar. I do not have a family member with bipolar and I can become manic without taking medications in the SSRI category. I am therefore identified as having atypical bipolar, a version of bipolar that does not fit into any other category of bipolar. Although I know of the existence of several types of bipolar, most people I talk to refer to themselves as having one of three types. The only other two types of bipolar that I have heard of are type 1 or type 2. Simply put, type 2 people suffer less severe manic episodes (hypomania) but both types can be susceptible to the same level of depression. In my experience, most people have this illness for one of two reasons. Some have a family member who has the disease; thus, they have a genetic predisposition. Second, there are those who have had a drug-induced episode; these result mainly from Prozac, Luvox, Celexa, Zoloft, or Paxil (SSRIs) in therapeutic doses, but also from Ritalin in abusive doses or from cocaine, heroin, marijuana, alcohol, or excessive caffeine. Every once in a while I will meet an individual who just has the disease without any one of these root causes being present or identifiable but usually one or more of these components combine to form the illness. To fit into one of the three categories (type 1, 2, atypical) of bipolar one can have experienced any or all of the antecedents mentioned above.

Most people diagnosed with any type of bipolar have the same general symptoms: mood changes between emotional highs (manic or hypo-manic episodes) and emotional lows (depressive episodes); because of these symptoms, the condition was commonly referred to as manic-depression. Later the name was changed to bipolar which means bi-two, polar-opposites. While in a high or manic state people are often susceptible to making poor decisions, agitation, increased sexual drive, excessive spending, weight loss or gain, rapid thoughts, sleeplessness, psychosis, concentration difficulties, increased productivity, and grandiose thoughts. Many people with a bipolar diagnosis experience manic episodes and hypomania. Some people experience only one condition or the other. Hypomania is a state similar to mania but less severe. While in a state of hypomania one usually experiences the same symptoms as mania but to a lesser extent. For example, a person who is hypo-manic may feel euphoric and lose some judgment but someone who is manic may feel so euphoric that they think that they are God and show such bad judgment that they may try to fly off a bridge because they believe in their godlike powers. When in the depressed state, they manifest opposite symptoms: increased appetite, decreased sexual drive, feelings of hopelessness and despair, lack of motivation, sadness, thoughts of suicide, and increased sleep. It is possible to be both manic and depressed at the same time. This type of emotional disposition is called a mixed episode. I clearly had a mixed episode when I was in Las Vegas so I will use that incident as an example. I was feeling extremely high in Vegas; I thought I was a multi-millionaire. I thought that I was going to get married to this stripper and my life was going to be great. At the same time I was confused and felt like my life was going to end, I felt that suicide was imminent though I did not have a reason to want to die. For example, I would be up in a building wondering whether or not I should jump off and kill myself and I would also be thinking about how fun it was to be in Vegas. A mixed state is very uncomfortable and very dangerous. People in a mixed state feel both manic and depressed at the same time. I both loved and hated myself at the same time.

My experience has been that I have never kept a specific diagnosis of one of the three types of bipolar for a very long time. I have also observed that many other people who have severe psychological problems tend to be re-analyzed and re-diagnosed several times. My diagnosis has been changed twice, from type 2 when I left the Pavilion in 2001, to atypical bipolar when I left the Pavilion after writing this book in 2002. Post-traumatic stress disorder was later added to my list of diagnoses from the most recent psychological evaluation done by my therapist. This is not to say that the entire diagnosis always changes but rather that the system is flawed. I do not believe in the use of specific labels. Specific labels undermine the relationship between the patient and the doctor. The patient is undermined because he/she will never be adequately cared for because he/she will never fit each specific element that accompanies the specific label of the disorder. The doctor is undermined because the doctor should be able to talk (and think to him or herself) about the person's personal needs instead of going through therapeutic motions that are already prescribed by a book or a teacher. There should be better dialogue between patient and doctor with the assumption that interpersonal work is better than applied therapeutic strategies learned through books and teaching. The broad diagnosis of bipolar is helpful because it gives both the patient and the doctor a place to start but the details of the illness should be something to be discovered and treated. Most of the great psychologists whom I have met treat patients as individuals, treating their specific thoughts and actions instead of following a regimented treatment plan.

I have met many people who have bipolar, especially through my affiliation with the Manic-Depressive and Depressive Association (MDDA). Often there will be several hundred people at these meetings, most diagnosed with bipolar. I have formed personal and intimate relationships with people who have been bipolar. I have treated children who have been bipolar.

The treatment for most bipolar people is pretty standard from a medical standpoint. Mood stabilizers are almost always prescribed; in fact, I have never heard of a doctor not prescribing a mood stabilizer to a bipolar patient. Although there are no medications used purely for this purpose, people call a medication a mood stabilizer if that is the purpose for which it is being used. As mentioned before, lithium is the most popular of these medications, but it is primarily an anti-seizure medication and an anticonvulsant.

There are many medications used as mood stabilizers. In addition to lithium, the main ones I see used are Depercote and Topamax. Each of these medications, especially Depercote and lithium, come in a variety of different forms, which include different release rates; for example, Escaleth is a slow-release version of lithium. Anti-psychotics are also used as mood stabilizers. People distinguish between mood stabilizers and anti-psychotics because the latter can be used to treat two different types of psychological illnesses. Someone may be on lithium for mood stabilization and Geadone (a new popular antipsychotic) for psychotic symptoms that may or may not be associated with bipolar. I know of a person who has a diagnosis of schizophrenia and bipolar type 1. This individual takes lithium to help control his mood from becoming either too high or too low. To treat his schizophrenia, he takes Geadone to help keep him from having hallucinations or delusions. I also know of another person who has a diagnosis of only bipolar type 2 who also takes Geadone but instead of helping him with schizophrenic issues he takes the Geadone to prevent him from having emotional highs and lows.

For depressive symptoms, antidepressants in the SSRI family are sometimes prescribed, but since most people who are bipolar get manic when put on this type of antidepressant, a doctor will be reluctant to prescribe an SSRI to any bipolar person. Most doctors, however, use other medicines, such as Wellbutrin, to treat depressive symptoms or prescribe lithium in conjunction with an SSRI.

Many medications, including lithium, require regular blood tests to determine toxicity and potency. In addition, there are various side effects even within limits of toxicity and potency that are considered safe. When I went on lithium, for instance, I gained weight and my hands shook a little. I could tolerate that, but when I started to feel slow or dulled, I decided that these were things that I could not tolerate. After that, I went on Depercote, which left me feeling dizzy and nauseous. I do not take a mood stabilizer, but I do take fish oil pills that have been proven in some studies to help regulate moods. This is against doctors' recommendations, however.

Although I could not tolerate the side effects of the medications, I know of many people who excel in life on medications. If you look on the web you will find many public figures who admit to being bipolar and who are also successful. Programs like the Pavilion are being started up all over the country. This is because there are so many people who have the thirty five thousand dollars to spend who are either bipolar or suffering from another serious psychological illness. Perhaps this is due to the fact that most of the richest people I have met, I have met in the hospital but I sincerely believe that the vast majority of all successful people are bipolar or in some way, psychologically unstable. I have met a lot of people in schools, clubs, through my family, etc… and only the most successful have been psychologically afflicted. I know of several famous musicians, whose names I cannot share, who are tremendously creative and still on mood stabilizers. I know of one Olympic athlete who is on lithium whose name I also cannot share. I know at least five billionaires from three countries who are bipolar. One is among the top fifty wealthiest people in this country; another is the richest person in another first-world country. I have met dozens of millionaires who are bipolar. Probably seventy percent of these people do very well while taking the medications, though others, like me, do not take any medications and do well too. This information probably sounds false but it is not. I am not saying that all the people I have written about in this paragraph are people I have met personally but I have met the majority of them. I embrace my illness. I think bipolar people are at a genetic disposition for success. Without it I would not be as creative. I do not want to get manic or depressed but I do like that sometimes I get racing thoughts and some of the other symptoms associated with hypomania. Most people that I know with this illness, even when on mood stabilizers, still experience dramatic mood changes. While depressed, I often become more creative. I go to darker places where I write interesting things. When I am high I go to a unique place too. I have known of depressed people becoming very compassionate and analytical, often finding solutions to other people's problems. I have seen manic people recruit clients and be more socially able.

I am not a doctor and my definition is derived from patients, input from other doctors, and my own beliefs and experience. The academic definitions, the axis on the psychological evaluation you might see on a bipolar report, really mean nothing. The disease is unique. The only constant I have seen in the illness is big emotional highs and big lows. Each person has different symptoms of mania and depression. I have met people who have been manic and thought they were Jesus Christ. I have met people who have thought that they could fly. Most of the people I meet with this illness, however, are between 15 and 35 and show similar symptoms. They are usually type 2 bipolar. These people usually love their highs and do not want to go on medications because they do not want to lose these elevated emotional states. Without it, though, they also get extremely low. Usually their depression manifests as suicidal ideation or as self-destructive actions that may result in suicide. Usually the problems type 2 people have associated with their manic states are substance abuse, impatience, hyper-sexuality, and general poor judgment (for example, speeding). Most doctors' explanations and those in books or on the Internet are inadequate. If anyone does want further information I suggest talking to a bipolar person. MDDA has groups for people who have friends and family affected by the illness, so anyone can attend those. MDDA exists in areas other than Massachusetts.

I find that in writing my definition of bipolar I am conflicted. Often things that I have read or that doctors have told me totally contradict my overall experience with bipolar. I am sure that a lot of doctors would disagree with what I am writing now and a lot of patients would too, but I think that the vast majority of patients and the good doctors would agree with me. Most doctors do not have this illness. I do.

Despite the limited insight into my problems that I gained at the Pavilion, I will try in this epilogue to explain why I did and thought what I wrote about in the free-style journal. I hope that some people who read my work will gain perception into themselves, their friends, and me even without this epilogue. It may be that some of my perceptions are flawed, and somewhere out there someone will read only the free-style journal and have truer perceptions into me, and/or an increased ability to understand themselves or a friend or family member. I would feel more comfortable if I left some mystery to myself, so I will remain somewhat enigmatic. With the last two sentences written, I am going to write this passage because I hope that some people can benefit through my understanding of why a bipolar person who suffers from post-traumatic stress disorder behaves and thinks in such a way.

I hope to help other people with bipolar or other mental disorders who worry about potential disasters by helping them understand where their thoughts are coming from. Once you understand where your thoughts are coming from, you are in a position to modify your behavior (if necessary), such as by avoiding particular people or situations, or to seek professional intervention (if necessary), and to do so in a more articulate manner.

I am obviously not always right, but maybe I will write something that will be able to help people. I honestly do want to help as many people as possible, not just the people suffering from the illness (and myself). I hope to give a sense of understanding and compassion to those close to the afflicted. Perhaps those around a bipolar or a PTSD victim will be able to prevent a crisis through understanding the nature of the illnesses. The ability to relate and show compassion towards other people is a necessary virtue for a better world. I know that when I feel bad, if someone simply shows me a little compassion and understanding I feel much better. I expect that many people, not just those with psychological illnesses, are comforted by others' understanding and compassion.

I enjoy challenges and I know that this epilogue is going to be the hardest part of the book. It is difficult for people to analyze themselves: or perhaps it would be fairer to say that it is hard for *me* to do this part because *I* have a hard time analyzing *myself*. It is difficult because it hurts me to think about all the bad things I have done, and about the fact that I did not have control over my behavior. I do not fully know why I did what I did and when I think about what I did last summer I feel sad. I can no longer hide from trying to put into words what made me do so many wicked things during the last three months, so I now have to choose where to start analyzing those thoughts and actions.

I choose to start with an overview of my life situation during the month leading up to the episode. I will then explain my emotions and behaviors around the time when I began to become symptomatic at the beginning of June. I will then explain the entire journal starting with the beginning of my free-style journal at the beginning of June 2002 and then I will go through the entire journal which ended in July. Because the other parts of the Introduction and Epilogue were not written while I was in a full manic state, it would not make any sense for me to analyze myself

184

when I have a normal thought process with normal actions. At the end of the epilogue I will write about my experiences of recovery that began in the months after the hospitalization.

At the beginning of May, I started to become increasingly angry. Ordinarily I am not an angry person, but when certain situations or thought processes occur I seem to begin going in a downward spiral often ending with a serious crisis. One of those times was during the late spring of 2002. I broke up with Emily in May. A month before I began writing I had technically broken up with Emily though we were still engaging in sexual activity. We stopped having sex in the middle of May until the documented incident in June where I wrote in a fury about her indiscretion with drugs in relation to the possibility of me contracting an STD. During May I was volunteering twice a week at the special needs school and getting ready for the paid position that I was going to begin in July. At the end of May, however, a full-time employee took a vacation and a supervisor approached me with the request that I start the paying position a month earlier by temporarily taking over the vacationing employee's position. I was happy to do so because the classroom I would begin paid work in adjoined the one where I was already working. I would not be far away from all the kids whom I had grown close to.

Leading up to the beginning of the job in June, I was happy because the weather was getting warmer and I had just been offered what I felt was a great position at the school. On the other hand, I was frustrated and lonely because Emily was gone, and I was afraid that I could not wake up at 5:45 AM in order to get to work on time. At the end of May I underwent a lot of classroom observation, and during this time I had to get used to waking up earlier than usual every weekday. I would have to continue waking up at 5:45 AM until the end of my work with the summer program.

I have never in my life woken up so early for more than a few days straight; in fact, when I was in high school I had to take days off from school because I was so tired. I am a night owl by nature, but that doesn't mean that I am a diehard partier; I am a geek, usually reading or writing until three in the morning and waking up at one in the afternoon. I love getting my sleep and I feel so good when I wake up late. My mother may be angry when I come downstairs, but I feel more in control. Now, suddenly, I had to change my sleeping pattern, and I think that I was unable to adjust. As happens with most sleep-deprived people, I began to grow irritable and show bad judgment and a lack of ability to think clearly. This was the beginning.

I believe that there is a strong chemical reaction that occurs that makes someone manic, but in my case it is drug-induced or situational rather than spontaneously occurring. When I was in Vegas I was taking the antidepressant Paxil. Although I knew it was making me wild, I liked the fact that I didn't need so much sleep and that I was socially outgoing. I did not think it was bad until I spent the 120k. A year later, in May 2002, I began having similar problems focusing on one issue and my thoughts would schism. I was also not getting enough sleep but this time my job was preventing me from sleep rather than the medication Paxil. In both cases the lack of sleep contributed heavily to inducing a manic episode. Another factor to the 2002 episode was the change of season. When the warm weather comes and

185

the day length increases, I get jovial, light-hearted, and more productive; the sunshine excites my entire persona. Both these elements—lack of sleep and increased light—combine for the volatile personality type, causing greater productivity but poorer judgment.

The most significant factor that pushed me into mania, however, was Emily. I loved her throughout the entire time I was writing the free-style journal, even when I wrote harshly about her. In almost all cases where people write poorly about someone they hate, they really love them; if I hated her I would not have wasted several hours over the course of several days insulting her. In order to hate someone you have to be deeply attached to them, love them, otherwise you just would not care enough to have hateful feelings. You have to love someone to hate them. Without obsession, neither love nor hate can be present. I was constantly thinking and obsessing about Emily. I thought about her for most of the day. There was a form of entertainment generated by my relationship with Emily. I filled my time with thoughts about her in order to distract myself. I loved fighting with Emily because without the fight my life is boring.

I also liked fighting because I am so used to it. I am used to fighting with both my family and my friends and, when I was young, with kids who bullied me. I was a timid person with no ability to perform in a social situation. My parents and friends did not know why I could not focus in school and on other people. When I was a child I was deeply effected by the trauma I experienced when I was raped. I should have talked to more people about my trauma so that I could have received more help. I have never been able to talk to my parents about being raped; I have always been too embarrassed. I still have not talked to my parents about being raped. Emily, who fought both consistently and with much fury, helped me to perpetuate this constant element in my life. Once you get used to a constant in life you miss it once it is gone. For instance, a middle class family may be very happy without excessive material possessions, but a wealthy person who loses his or her wealth may become miserable. I am used to being hurt. Being hurt is all I know about relationships, especially sexual relationships. I do not realize these thoughts consciously, but subconsciously I am used to being severely hurt as an introduction to sexual relationships. As a result, I have also gotten used to fighting and now, with Emily gone, I found that I missed it. The human mind works in complex ways and after I was raped I needed other people to hurt me like Steve did and Emily filled the role of being an abuser quite well. Now that she is gone my mind makes me crave the abuse despite my obvious understanding that it is not healthy to perpetuate a vicious cycle of hurt. This is a key area of work with Dr. Frazier, understanding why I need people to hurt me so that I can eliminate that need.

Without Emily I was alone. At the beginning of our relationship I had threatened to break up with her many times. However, it was not until the beginning of May that I told her "I want to break up." I did not think she would break up with me, at least without an argument, because she seemed so attached to me, but she simply said "Fine." I immediately missed her, but at the time I would not admit that to myself. Instead of admitting my frustration towards her I kept it all inside. I did not want to admit that I loved Emily. After I broke up with Kim I had decided I would never fall in love again, instead I thought that I would marry some rich, pretty girl.

I was drawn to Emily because she was pretty and wealthy. She also seemed to be a good person, and she provided so much companionship after I had felt alone for so long. I had not dated anyone for a year and Emily and I spent all our time together. I now realize, however, that I would never have fallen in love with her if she had not hurt me. I fell in love with Emily because she turned out to be a bad person. She turned out to be someone like Steve, the man who raped me. Emily wanted sex from me but she did not care about me emotionally. I viewed Emily in the same way as Steve on a subconscious level, however, in the past few months through therapy I have been able to understand that I have subconscious thoughts like this one. Now I am able to identify why I loved Emily, but during the relationship I could not. I have never really wanted to hurt Steve except when I get manic. Usually, I want to help him because I know that no good comes from pain. If Steve were helped, then he would pose less of a threat to society, and perhaps through studying his case and similar ones psychologists could gain insights that would help reduce the incidence of child rape and abuse.

I loved Emily because she always found a way to hurt me emotionally. She would make me cry and make me vulnerable. Emily could inflict more damage on me than I could do to myself. She exposed a weakness that I was not even aware of having; she did this because she felt vulnerable. She kept me emotionally weak so that I would be afraid. She lowered my self-esteem so that I would not feel confident enough to leave her. Emily always threatened to kill herself if I left. Emily always hated me as much as she loved me. I liked that.

Emily and I broke up for reasons that require a lot of insight, and I would be presumptuous to state my perceptions into why she does what she does. With the previous sentence's disclaimer, I will be presumptuous anyway. I am going to make assumptions about Emily because in the free-style journal I do not feel that I portray her accurately or establish her as a three-dimensional character. The main reason for her deep love/hatred towards me, I believe, was her relationship with her father. Emily's dad was rarely around, and when he was, Emily would try and try to misbehave to make him punish her. What she really wanted was guidance and discipline, but her father gave her neither. Emily's first boyfriend was crazy. He told her what to do about everything and Emily willingly followed. She needed direction. Emily felt as though through his control she would be safe because she could not make any mistakes. He followed her around, told her how to dress and who to talk to. She asked me to do the same for her, to tell her exactly what to do. At first she told me it was because her last boyfriend was abusive and she needed the control, but that is untrue. She needed the guidance that her father never gave her. She was constantly petrified about the prospect of a day alone, a day away from me. She was scared that she would cheat on me, scared she would do drugs or get into a fight, and in fact she did do these things if I did not spend enough time with her. Emily is one of the most frightened people I have ever met, and she is not afraid without reason. She knew the difference between right and wrong; she just needed that attention and guidance.

I often gave her suggestions to the point that I was at times arrogant and so we worked together well. If she asked me a question I told her what I thought she should do. I fell into the trap of being Emily's surrogate father. Emily hates her father for not taking care of her and giving her that direction. She is justified in hating him for this. I became the guidance figure for Emily; I also became the new object of hate. As the result of my experiences with Emily I no longer give people advice. I only ask questions, trying to help the individual come to his or her own conclusions. I will never give direction again. I have learned this not only from Emily but also from work. You let the person get a solution to a problem without guidance or suggestion. You can only help answer questions and give support.

Emily was someone who yearned for attention, discipline, and guidance, but also for someone to hate as much as the father who had failed to give her these things. Since her father never taught her to think or act independently, she will always break up with passive men and always pursue bad men, men who will hurt her in order to get her to do what they want. Speaking of one nice man she had dated, Alan, she would state that she broke up with him because she was afraid she would hurt him, which was true, but she was much more afraid that nice people would not tell her what to do; without that she was open to disaster. She would date bad people for two reasons, the main one being that she hoped that they would control her and the second one, more noble perhaps, being that she did not care if she hurt a bad person. I anticipate that she will continue to be dissatisfied with her life until she becomes more conscious of her subconscious wants and needs and begins to modify her behavior through therapy.

In my free-style journal I wrote about how she uses Alcoholics Anonymous and Narcotics Anonymous as a source of meeting sexual partners. That is not true. Emily loves NA and AA because they are regimented and structured. There is so much black and white in those organizations. In NA and AA you follow extremely rigid guidelines of personal conduct and at the beginning of each meeting you read the same lines, about how one substance is too much and a million, not enough. Emily is very susceptible to cult influences. I sincerely believe that NA and AA are cult organizations and I think that there are alternative programs that are healthier. Everyone I have ever met who has participated in these groups believes that he or she can only be close to an addict, believe that only addicts understand each other, and let their "sponsor" (another member of the program who looks out for them) tell them what to do. To me these aspects brought together represent a cult and I have seen people recover in alternative programs.

Obviously, Emily plays a major role in my writing and when I am not writing about her I am being moved by the anger I feel towards her. I am not stating that she was the only reason I had this episode, but she had a major impact on me during that period. Would I ever date Emily again? No. Would I ever have sex with her again? I probably will. Emily to me was a terrible person, like Steve, but she was someone I could potentially cure. I wish that I could have cured Steve and a part of me wants to cure Emily so that I can feel like I cured Steve. If I cured Steve then he would no longer be a threat to me now and he would no longer be a threat to anyone else. I am still scared that Steve is going to come for me. So I helped

Emily, despite the pain she inflicted, and it made me feel a little better when month after month she would tell me how she was feeling better. I do not only hate her; when I dated her I loved her and so did my family. I said mean things about her after my frustrations mounted. She served an important role in my life and therefore warranted an enormous amount of my attention. I knew that she would cheat on me and hurt me. I needed that. Maybe I only needed her and I never loved her. Maybe I do not know what love is at all.

The situation that prompted me to viciously verbally attack her was when she indicated to me that she would no longer hurt me. When I knew she was out of my life and we could no longer play painful games, I cursed her more because without intending to she had inflicted the ultimate act of love. Emily broke the cycle of pain that I needed so badly. She brought my love for her to a new level by making me hate her so much. She made me curse at her because after we had sex she cried and told me that she did not love me anymore. Despite the way I portray it in the free-style journal, I was most upset because she said she did not love me anymore. She brought the game to a more intense level. After everything we had gone through I never thought she would stop loving me and for each mean word I wrote about her I wiped tears from my eyes. I had to be tough and manly, so I attacked her instead of stating how sad I was about her falling away from me. I should have written about both feelings.

I loved Emily very much and she was good for me in certain ways. In my speech for an award I recently received for excellent work at my special needs school, I thanked her, and I really do have no ill feelings towards her. I no longer need her specifically, but I still need someone like her, someone who will hurt me. So even though I know I have grown, I still have a way to go. I would like to be attracted to girls who will not hurt me. I have seen Emily recently and she is not ugly as my verbal attack indicated and I still honestly worry about her psychological condition, but I do not think I can help her. Recently I tried to help her only to have her completely sever communications. It was probably my fault; I am still upset and there is no question that I said things to her that I should not have said. I think that we will both need help if we ever resume communication.

Again, I will try to pick up from where I left off. I was all ready to start my new position in the last week of May 2002 when several elements came together that pushed me over the edge into a manic state: I was sleep-deprived and had been dumped by someone I needed, and the warm weather was making me feel grandiose. Still, I was doing very well at work and was never angry towards the kids. I know that even if I had not had my writing as an outlet I still would not have been in any way short with those children. I decided originally that I was going to begin a book to showcase all of my creative abilities. I wanted to use poetry, prose, drawings, and photography. I had a tremendous amount of creative energy and I did not need sleep, which are two classic warning signs of an impending manic episode. I wanted to produce a piece of work that would be torn apart by the critics in the hope that there would be one aspect of it that some critic would like and that I could use as the basis for a more calculated and thoughtful piece of work on that subject. Now I understand that I have done something totally different. I may have started with that idea but I did not finish it. In order for me to write and produce visual art that spanned my artistic spectrum, I became impulsive. Impulsivity is an easily misunderstood word, and in my case I use it to mean letting words and actions go from emotion to action. My writings are not calculated; they are edited but they are emotions.

When I began writing I quickly fell into a trap of thinking about my first abuser, Steve. I was irritable because of my inability to clearly understand whether I loved Emily or not, and I was frustrated because, in general, I always want to do more and am unsatisfied even when functioning on a high level. Steve has had such a major effect on my life that there is not one aspect of my life that has not been affected by him. I believe that I made my relationship with Emily in order to identify with my abuser Steve. I can remember little of my youth. I remember Steve holding my own sword up to my chest and telling me, "I can kill you at any time I want." I can remember him stating his ability to kill me with ease several times before he began to slowly work up to his eventual rape of me. He scared me and made me believe he was going to kill me. He also made me sure of my sexuality. I know that I am not gay. A lot of young people in this society experiment with others of the same sex or have homosexual urges. Most young people, however, determine their sexual orientation through experimentation, not through rape. Many boys, for example, will masturbate together and from that experience determine whether they are gay or not. Women have similar experiences. I never questioned my heterosexuality after the incident with Steve.

Regardless, the feelings I had when I was a child continue to manifest in the feelings that I have today, feelings that I understand having and cannot help but have. Identifying with the abuser means that either I or someone I am close to plays the role of the abuser towards me, or I play it towards them. Again I am getting way ahead of myself because my most important identification with the abuser came when I was cut. I feel like I deserve to be hurt. The police officer echoed Steve; both men wanted to forcibly rape me, be violent towards me. I hate myself and I am embarrassed to have engaged in sexual acts with a man, especially since I ejaculated with him. The embarrassment is so strong inside me that I wish I were dead. Everyone knows that feeling of embarrassment that is so intense that they wish they could just disappear. I feel that way all the time. My embarrassment serves as a catalyst to my rage; I want to kill myself but then I feel guilty because I do not want to hurt anyone; then my guilt turns into frustration and I get extremely angry and impulsive. That is why I spent one hundred grand in Vegas: I was angry about not being able to kill myself, so I made a subconscious attempt to make it more acceptable to kill myself. If I spent all that money and then killed myself, people would already hate me and care less about losing me.

This is the direction that the free-style journal took. I was feeling some anger at the beginning, but when I began to write about Steve I began radiating only rage. I am not a rage-filled person, but I do sometimes feel extreme anger. Ever since Steve abused me, I have looked for others to do the same. I have felt as though I have deserved it and I have felt so much shame for what I did with him. The dream I relate in my free-style journal is an expression of innocence being torn from its womb; the little girl screaming represents my innocence leaving. In reality I was older than the little girl when I was raped, but the dream represents the beginning of the loss of innocence, the loss of innocence not only by rape but by going through puberty. The buildings of the hospital represent my attempts to get better, and through these attempts comes the realization that in order to feel better I have to develop a deeper ability to perceptualize. To understand myself better, I enter the basement, the heart of the building, as I enter my own heart in search of answers. The children who are being tortured and are too young to have an orgasm represent myself. They represent my fear of understanding that I must have enjoyed some kind of sexual pleasure in order to have had orgasms with Steve. The children enjoy being tortured because it disturbs me to remember having enjoyed ejaculation when Steve forced me to have sex. The fact that most of the images are of girls being raped by men represents my idea that it would have been more acceptable if I were a woman. I would feel less sexually confused if I had been raped by a woman. The children brutally show me how terrible everything is. At that age I should not have had orgasms with another person. I was too young. I should have gotten to know myself through masturbation first before I let someone else touch me. Children learn to become comfortable with their own bodies through masturbation. One must feel comfortable with his or her own body and how it works before having sex with someone else. I did not have the chance to learn by myself, in my own time, how to feel comfortable with my own body. It was Steve who taught me how my body worked, Steve who taught me how to ejaculate quickly or slowly. I had no chance to develop my own sexual fantasies. I needed to establish on my own a basic idea of sexual desires. Instead, Steve confused me about everything relating to relationships and sexuality.

Blood plays a dominant role in my free-style journal and especially in this dream. Blood represents many things to different people; to me it represents life. In the dream the blood is life lost, or leaving. The blood represents all the childhood memories that I lost, all the parts of my life that I have not enjoyed because of the rapes. The children smile right before they die because I wish I had died on one of those hot summer nights when I was raped. When I get to the basement, the pit of my despair, I am closer to hell and am able to see how my disease has grown inside me. I get to see that Steve made me destroy women, I get to see myself destroy Emily and Kim physically. Their physical decay, with considerable attention focused on their vaginal areas, represents the mental trauma that I believe I inflicted on them. I never told Kim I was raped, but I did tell Emily, a long time after I first had sex with her. In fact, she was the first person I ever told about what had happened to me. This was extremely difficult for me because I feel diseased by having participated in such covert and socially unacceptable sexual acts. I feel as though I passed along my disease —both my physical disease and my psychological disease—to Kim and Emily.

I cry every time I wake up from this dream because I have learned to understand its meaning and I find it disturbing. Insight does not always provide a solution. I did not have insight, though, during the time I was writing my free-style journal. If

I had been able to perceptualize and use my insights productively I would not have a massive debt and a foot-long, inch-wide scar on my chest.

Sometimes insight develops only after one acts on impulse. I feel this is what happened in my case. Our perception is what makes us, as humans, great, With the ability to perceptualize and then develop skills to use those understandings we can gain insight that enables us to solve all types of problems. Creativity only exists because of perception. It is through creativity that we develop cures for diseases and find alternatives to wars. Creative people often are able to think of more than one solution to a problem. It is therefore not unfair to conclude that if there are many potential solutions to a problem then perhaps a war can be avoided through a creative way to propitiate.

I did not know why I behaved how I did in the months of May, June, and July until several weeks after my hospital discharge. I did not understand what was wrong with Emily until after I had lost my opportunity to tell her. Even after I got out of the hospital, in November, I spent two thousand dollars at a strip club that I was trying to save for a car and to help get this book published, but like some other situations in my life I only gain insight into my actions after they are completed. The difference between now (December) and then (the month of June) is that in June I had no perceptive abilities. I was so completely caught in the rapture of abusing myself. Emily made me seek pain, as I have been doing ever since Steve abused me.

After the part about my dream I included a group of love poems, all written before I wrote this free-style journal. I added these after I was released from the hospital because I wanted to provide a more balanced picture of myself. I am not so filled with hatred that I do not have any capacity to love, as these love poems demonstrate. The free-style journal also includes many references to my feelings about this society and my culture. I hate society; I hate it because it hates me. Society hates me because I have a mental disorder and because I had sex with a man. I hate society because I think it is cold towards people of different lifestyles and ethnic backgrounds. In America there are still strong racial prejudices and it is an undeniable fact that the majority of people, if they knew my story and my diagnosis, would stay as far away from me as possible. They would not take time away from their busy days of MTV or "The West Wing" to make the effort to understand me. I guess I am angry now, but everyone involved in my book-writing process has told me to put a damper on my rage so that people can understand my own three-dimensional nature. I have begun taking their advice because I feel many things besides anger. I love the children I worked with. I love some of my co-workers. I love my family. I have healthy, well-rounded relationships in my life. I have a lot to be thankful for and a lot of people to thank.

I hope that underneath all the rage in my free-style journal, people will be able to understand and relate to some of my ideas about religion and society. I understand psychosis well and none of my writing is psychotic. Some of the religious information is extremely academic, and some of the references are not only complicated but contain multiple meanings. I would suggest that to understand my religious satire and commentary one should read a general religious anthology,

Dante's *Divine Comedy*, and the Old Testament of the Bible. I do, however, use some very obscure references. For example, I use the words "heart's lake," which many people would think was a word combination that I invented for the sole purpose of making a point in my book; in actuality the heart's lake is an anatomical term used in the 12th and 13th centuries in Europe. The heart's lake was believed to be a passage inside the human heart from where the emotion of fear originated; at that time it was generally believed that all feelings originated in the heart, but specific to the heart's lake was the feeling of fear. The free-style journal is full of many such references that I used to try to convey abstract ideas.

The two books above are the main sources of my information, but they are not the only ones. I use information from Darwin's *Origin of Species,* Machiavelli's *The Prince, Art of War,* and *Discourses,* and Freud's *Interpretation of Dreams.* I reference Rousseau's *Social Contract* and use ideas from Martin Luther's original letters translated. I have used as inspiration Marlowe's *Dr. Faustus* and some of Shakespeare's plays, in particular *The Tempest*, as well as Nietzsche's *On the Genealogy of Morals.* I use some of the ideas I found in Max Weber's and Karl Marx's original transcripts. I sometimes allude to Greek and Roman mythology, most of which comes from Dante but also from scattered books about ancient mythology, including Robert Graves' *The Greek Myths: Complete Edition.*

I have read and studied Vincent Bugliosi and Curt Gentry's *Helter Skelter,* I have read most of Kay Redfield Jameson's books and Elizabeth Wurlitzer's, I have read *The Bell Jar* and *Girl Interrupted* too. I am not bragging about how many books I have read, but to dismiss my free-style journal as a bunch of random utterings from a despondent mental patient is ridiculous. I do not regard myself as a genius but rather would hope that after reading of my sources of inspiration, people may either be motivated to read some of them on their own or to try to decipher some of my more complex writing in a more systematic way. Most people with a college education are familiar with these books and by knowing which books I specifically reference I provide a valuable resource to understanding my material and I also make myself look less like a nut.

In addition to the great works of literature and philosophy listed above, I have also been influenced by many contemporary writers and musicians. These include Korn, Nine Inch Nails, Tupac Shakur, The Doors, Jimmy Hendrix, Sublime, Kurt Cobain, Janis Joplin, The Rolling Stones, Johnny Cash, Tool, and many other musicians who are just as lucid and insightful as many of the old great thinkers. Some artists in particular, such as Jonathan Davis of Korn, used to help get me through a lot of the toughest times in my life. If Mr. Davis had not shown me that rage was an acceptable outlet for how I was feeling I would have killed myself. He also showed me that I could use my rage constructively. I do not want to be redundant but I would like to thank him again.

Another symptom of bipolar illness is to lose track of one's thoughts and go all over the place. I demonstrated this throughout my free-style journal. I hurt when I talk about Steve and so I have described him only briefly, even though I do believe his actions and influences could benefit from a fuller description. I wish I could provide a better account of his influences on me, but I have forgotten a lot of what he did. I am also still trying to understand how he influenced me. Besides, he did not share anything with me ever and he stopped talking to me after he started raping me.

There is little else that I can write about Steve. One day Steve was acting really weird towards me and not sharing any cookies while he was eating them right in front of me, and my mom told him he was fired. Steve cried and begged for his job and then he left. I remember how frightened my mom was, and I was only numb. He was hired by my mother and father to be the household nanny. His job included watching over the children while my parents were gone and keeping the house looking neat. While in the position, he lived in our house in my bedroom. That is where most of the abuse occurred. I believe I was around ten when I was abused. I believe that he lived in our house for two months though I could be wrong about both of the previous statements. My mother always had her doubts about Steve. Several months after he raped me she asked me if he had raped me; I said no. When she was questioning me about Steve raping me she told me that Steve had been abused by his father. That is almost all I remember about him.

Throughout the free-style journal I write about several times that I engage in dangerous or unusual behavior. I do this because during some periods in my life I like the feeling of physical pain and I only feel comfortable when people are mad or hurting me. The more people are mad at me, the more of an excuse I have to kill myself. In my suicide note I can write about how everyone hated me and justify my suicide. I am so used to pain. I have overdosed three times and cut, stabbed, tattooed, and pierced myself numerous times. My skin has turned paper white and I have lost my ability to speak while my parents took me to get my stomach pumped. I tried to die but my mom knew I was sick, I was close to death. Recently when I was cut, I was cut to the bone, through muscle, through tendons. Pain is a feeling, and any feeling is better than none. Sometimes I get so depressed that I cannot feel anything. I think that I get depressed like that because it is a coping mechanism that I used to defend myself both from the action and the resulting thoughts from being tortured and raped. I have spent a large part of my life trying to numb myself. I try to numb myself from bad memories of pain. In the process of numbing myself I have made myself more flat. I am so used to feeling nothing that now I have trouble feeling anything. When I hurt myself I feel something, and the something that I do feel is familiar. Most of the time, however, I feel numb, numb because I had to protect myself from feeling the shame of being raped.

When I am depressed I am feeling the depressive side of my bipolar. I sleep all day, stay in my room feeling nothing and wanting to die. The manic side is more profound in my free-style journal. I am happy but agitated, walking a precarious line between success on one side and chaos and overload on the other.

I know that I have written it before but I will say it again. Usually I do not feel either depressed or manic. Most of my life is normal. All of last year up until I got the full-time job I was content. Emily and I had regular problems but overall I was happy with the relationship. My mood was consistent and positive, month after month, and I enjoyed participating in all kinds of activities. Now I am in a recovery process where I am trying, with the help of professionals, to gain insight in order to understand what went wrong and how I can live a more enjoyable, incident-free life. I am in the process of applying for readmission to college, and I am looking for a new girlfriend in night school classes. I hope that in another month or so I will regain my footing. I want to demonstrate that my moods and behaviors are under control.

I hope that (partially through this book) I will gain the insight necessary to avoid both manic and depressive episodes. I do not want to use medication and so I stopped. I understand that I am always going to have to deal with greater mood swings in my life than most people, but I am ready to adjust my life.

When I drove fast in my car I wanted to die; I wanted to go down in flames so that someone would notice me. I modified my car because I, like all men, want a bigger penis. I have a big penis but again like all men I want it bigger. I modified my car not because I feel that my penis is too little to be effective but because I want the biggest damn penis in the known universe. I also know that too big of a penis hurts a woman. So I show off my penis with my car. Girls talk with each other and compare the size of their boyfriend's or husband's penis. Oftentimes they do not even mention the anatomy; they just talk about his intelligence or big muscles or money or fast car. Many components put together compensate for the penis. My car extends my penis without hurting the girl, just like my intelligence and money. I cannot be the greatest at any one thing, but I can have many great attributes that add together to give me the biggest penis, i.e. make me the most desirable man.

In other words I was competing with the other men and one way to compete is to have the best stuff, the fastest car. Women compete vaginally with intelligence for creation and nurture, men compete with muscles and material possessions/ success. Mother always existed for millions of years. Father only existed for the last five thousand years or less. People used to think that women became pregnant by the winds or by eating beans or swimming. Humans and animals just thought sex was fun but did not find the connection with childbirth until later. Therefore, women care for creation, men care about having the biggest penis/competition. My car being that fast would make me more desirable. Now I have skewed my point, which in reality is two different points. My first point is that modifying the car is to compete with other men. My second point is that driving fast is to die because I hate myself.

I write directly to females who are reading my free-style journal. I was so lonely during this time that I was trying any way I could to elicit a female response. Ever since Steve abused me I have had difficulty making male friends. The reason is simple and Freudian: I am afraid of other men's penises. I am afraid that one of them will once again use it against me as Steve did when I was a child. I made an exception last year when I became friends with an older male who was a police officer; I thought he would be safe. After he tried to rape me I felt like this world truly does hate me. I still do. My male friends are all superficial except for the one who cut me; I will discuss him below.

Everyone I give the free-style journal to reads it very fast, then stops at the same place, right after I attack Emily. I think it is because I am so full of rage that the reader needs a break. Although that part of the free-style journal was precipitated by her use of an unclean needle and our subsequent unprotected sex, the real reason I attacked her, as I wrote earlier, was because of my conflicting feelings of love and hatred for her combined with the fact that it had become clear to me that she no longer wanted me. I hated her for deserting me, and what pushed me over the edge and made me so mad that I flipped out was when she told me she did not want me back. I finally understood that she did not love/hate me anymore, and I thought I would be alone forever. She had become indifferent towards me, whereas I wanted her to continue to hate/love me. I had to vent my anger somewhere, and I did that through my writing, but my behavior also changed. In the weeks before this I had begun engaging in high-risk behavior, but now I began doing things that were life-threatening. I could not leave my house without the real prospect that I would not come back home. This is when I almost killed myself by driving recklessly and when my friend stabbed me. I will dedicate the last part of this epilogue to this second incident since it is crucial to understanding my illness.

To have a total understanding of me it is also important to understand both Kim and Jess, it would take a whole book to talk about Kim. Jess did not play a big enough role in my life to warrant further explanation in this book. Obviously Emily played a massive role in my life and I would consider writing a book about her. The prospect, however, of me writing another book specifically about any of these three women (Emily, Kim, and Jess) is great because I think we lived fascinating lives together, and even if we did not, their inner lives were most definitely interesting.

Back to my friend who cut me. His name is Eric, and I have known him for years, since before I met Steve. Unfortunately I cannot divulge any personal information about this person because I do not want him to go to prison. I also do not want Eric to sue me for presenting him as a criminal. I have written much about my unwanted search for someone to treat me like Steve, and this friend has consistently played this role in my life. My friend made me hurt badly, just as Steve had. He scares me with his dangerous activities and draws me into various uncomfortable situations. I developed a friendship with a person like Eric because I needed a person like Steve. When someone has a big impact on your life it is hard to let them go. This is why I found someone to act as Steve.

During June and July 2002 my psychological condition deteriorated to such a point that I needed someone to inflict pain upon me. The few (maybe six or seven) people who have read my free-style journal tell me I come across as a person full of rage and hatred. They are right. I was full of rage and hatred and the person I hated most was myself, although I was too short-sighted and manic to understand this. I hated myself for sounding mean and arrogant and pretentious. I hated myself so much that, finally, I tried to kill myself. I went about this in a ritualistic manner: I grew long sideburns and long hair, got really tan, and whitened my teeth. Then I set up a lighting stage with all kinds of photographic equipment; I planned to die in front of the world.

I wanted to end this book on a positive point and so I am going to explain how Steve, through his torture to me, created someone with heightened levels of empathy and caring. It has been difficult and painful to write this Epilogue. Sometimes I have ended up getting drunk because in examining my life I realize how much pain I have caused other people and how much pain I have caused myself. I read through this passage and see how much I hate myself. Despite my ability to understand and interpret many of my actions in a very complex way, I am still unable to elevate my emotional levels and create good strategies to avoid future disasters. I am still afraid of men. At times I am still unable to maintain control over my emotions and behaviors. Then I look at how far I have come, from a scared boy to an adult with rewarding relationships. I look at how through understanding myself I have been able to avert disaster. I can think about all the times I sat bleeding, including the time last summer, and I decided to get help instead of die. When I was young I could not speak in front of a group of ten people. I went friendless through most of high school. I constantly fought with my family, breaking household objects in rage.

I am trying hard to understand my problems, but that does not mean that I might not make the same mistakes. My perceptions of how my trauma has affected me have helped me understand a lot about how to control my life. As terrible as my last relationship may seem, I was able to identify the reasons for the problem and determine that I would be hurting myself to maintain the relationship with Emily. I recently have been in positions to reinitiate a relationship with her but I have chosen not to due to my understanding of her and of the dynamics of a relationship with her. Our relationship lasted only a few months, but I learned a lot from it. By contrast, in the past, I have had relationships lasting several years with women with worse problems of substance abuse and mental illness. I have gradually slowed down and have now stopped a trend of dating people who will hurt me. The process has been slow, but I should not confuse a gradual change with no change. I also have been avoiding high-risk situations. Despite my terrible lack of judgment in the photo shoot and the three or four incidents that I wrote about in the free-style journal, I have come a long way. My life is no longer full of lucky escapes, such as from the cops when I am drunk driving or speeding.

All these areas of progress should not be underestimated, and the fact that I can identify the role that Steve played in creating an adult who is dangerous to himself is especially helpful. I now have the ability to question my actions before I do them. These days I work hard helping people who were or are treated the way I was. I help children who have been raped and abused or who suffer from severe mental illnesses. I was hurt by Steve. I grew up to not want anyone to be hurt like that again. I do not wish to sound conceited, but I am proud of the work I do. I do not think that most people have the patience to work with a child who not only verbally refuses to work but becomes verbally and physically assaultive. I get paid nine dollars an hour for this work. My family may be rich but I am not showered in gifts. I do not have a large trust fund that I access money from. After my trip to Vegas I declared bankruptcy. After I modified my car my father made me pay back every cent to him. I am still paying. My parents have not set me up in some lavish apartment and I do not wear designer clothes. I have had to pay for publishing this book with money that I have earned working with the children. The only thing that my parents pay for is my psychological help. I have been an expensive patient and I appreciate what my family has done for me, including the fact that my parents have instilled in me a sense of independence.

Steve created a circle. I was raped and tortured, but rather than causing me to do the same, I grew up to develop tremendous empathy and sympathy towards people. Now, having reached the same age as Steve was when he abused me, I have begun to make a career out of helping others who have been hurt. I sit down with children at the school where I teach with the knowledge that I am able to help them in a very special way. Because I have experienced so much trauma, I can easily relate to the children and can therefore provide more effective support and direction. By raping me, Steve created someone who will spend the rest of his life donating time and effort to helping others.

ISBN 141202188-X

9 781412 021883

Made in the USA